The Practice of Strategic
Environmental Assessment

The Practice of Strategic Environmental Assessment

Riki Thérivel and Maria Rosário Partidário

EARTHSCAN

Earthscan Publications Ltd, London

First published in the UK in 1996 by
Earthscan Publications Limited

A catalogue record for this book is available from the British Library

ISBN: 1 85383 373 8

Typesetting and page design by PCS Mapping & DTP, Newcastle upon Tyne
Printed and bound by Biddles Ltd, Guildford and Kings Lynn
Cover design by Elaine Marriott

For a full list of publications please contact:
Earthscan Publications Limited
120 Pentonville Road
London N1 9JN
Tel. (0171) 278 0433
Fax: (0171) 278 1142
Email: earthinfo@earthscan.co.uk

Earthscan is an editorially independent subsidiary of Kogan Page Limited and publishes in
association with the WWF-UK and the International Institute for Environment and
Development.

Contents

Part II: Sectoral SEAs

Part III: Seas of Comprehensive/Area-based Plans

Part IV: SEAs of Policies

Part V: Conclusions

Author Information

Eva Asplund is a regional planner at the Regional Planning Division of the Royal Institute of Technology in Stockholm.

Dr Kevin Bradley is and environmental scientist, and works as an administrator with the European Commission's Environment, Nuclear Safety and Civil Protection Directorate-General (DG XI).

Ian Campbell is a senior environmental analyst at the Environment Bureau, Policy Branch, Agriculture and Agri-Food Canada.

Ann Dom is a physicist and an environmental consultant who has been involved in SEA for the transport sector for several years. She was project leader of the SEA for the European High Speed Train Network.

Dr Tuija Hilding-Rydevik is an assistant professor at the Division of Land and Water Resources in the Royal Institute of Technology in Stockholm.

Ram Khadka is the coordinator for the EIA Programme at IUCN–The World Conservation Union/Nepal in Kathmandu, Nepal.

Dr Volker Kleinschmidt is executive director of the environmental research consultancy Pro Terra Team, Division EIA Research Centre, based in Dortmund.

Dr Maria Rosário Partidário is an assistant professor at the Department of Sciences and Environmental Engineering at the New University of Lisbon, with a PhD on SEA (1992) from Aberdeen University. She is currently working on several SEA research projects.

John Rumble is a town planner for Hertfordshire County Council. He is a member of the team that established the sustainability concepts for Hertfordshire's structure plan.

Harri Seppanen is chief forest officer at the Forest Management and Utilisation Development Project/FINNIDA in Kathmandu, Nepal.

Uttam S Shrestha is Programme Officer for the EIA Programme at IUCN–The World Conservation Union/Nepal in Kathmandu, Nepal.

Lorene L Sigal, retired, was until 1995 a research staff member and group leader in the Environmental Analysis Section of the Environmental Sciences Division at Oak Ridge National Laboratory. She led a number of projects that assess compliance with the US National Environmental Policy Act and other environmental regulations (eg, the Clean Air Act) and led a UN Task Force on applying the principles of EIA to policies, plans, and programmes.

Amy O Skewes-Cox is a land use planner and principal of her own consulting firm called Land/Water Consultants based in Berkeley and Markeleeville, California. The firm specialises in environmental impact analyses for land-use plans and new developments.

Riki Thérivel is a senior lecturer at Oxford Brookes University's School of Planning. She is joint course leader for the MSc course in Environmental Assessment and Management, and a research associate in the Impacts Assessment Unit.

Rob Verheem is currently Deputy secretary of the Dutch EIA Commission. He has worked at the European Commission in Brussels, and at the Ministry of the Environment.

Dieter Wagner is a city and regional planner in Köln.

J Warren Webb is a research staff member in the Environmental Analysis Section of the Environmental Sciences Division at Oak Ridge National Laboratory. In the area of SEA, he served on a UN Task Force on applying the principles of EIA to policies, plans and programmes and has helped prepare reports on hydropower policy and environmental analysis of trade agreements.

Acknowledgements

This book is the joint work of many individuals. Each case study chapter was written by (very busy) SEA practitioners to a very high standard and very tight deadlines. We are enormously grateful to all the contributors for their excellent and – every editor's dream – prompt contribution. Jonathan Sinclair Wilson, our editor at Earthscan, gave us ongoing support, and ensured that the book was published as rapidly as possible. This collaborative effort has meant that the book is both practice-oriented and as up-to-date as possible.

The book has also indirectly benefitted from many other peoples' input. The idea for the book arose during a conference on SEA organised by Janet Brand and Fiona Walsh at Crieff (Scotland) in March 1995. Stewart Thompson collaborated in a research project on SEA and nature conservation for English Nature, to which Brian Smith, Keith Porter and Paul Buckley gave invaluable advice; much of Chapters 1 and 3 is based on that research. This and related research involved interviewing, running courses with, and receiving questionnaire responses from hundreds of SEA practitioners and local authority planners in the UK. Particular thanks to Martin Baxter, Chris Ferrary, Norman Lee, Arthur Keller, Peter Nelson, Karen Raymond, Bill Sheate and Nick Simon. Thanks also to John Glasson, Elizabeth Wilson, Joe Weston and the other wonderful members of Oxford Brookes University's Impacts Assessment Unit for a pleasant and supportive working environment.

Our acknowledgements must cut across continent frontiers. A research project on key issues in SEA, developed in Canada under NATO and the Canadian Environmental Assessment Agency, provided important insights on new approaches and existing realities; aspects of Chapter 1 and much of Chapter 2 are based on that research. Discussions conducted as part of this research with various people, and particularly with Patrice LeBlanc, Ray Clark and Barry Sadler are gratefully acknowledged.

We also thank those people whom we wish could have been on our list of contributors. Brett Odgers of EPA Australia made great efforts to chase some of the best Australian environmental assessment professionals to produce a chapter on the Australian Timber Inquiry but, due to time constraints, had to withdraw a few months later. Thanks also to Jenny Dixon for productive discussions on the New Zealand approach to SEA, which this book cannot include because of a lack of practical examples.

The book was pulled together in Oxford and Lisbon, and coordinated almost solely by telephone, fax and mail. We thank each other for the patience, hard work, enthusiasm and goodwill involved in co-editing a book when based hundreds of kilometres apart. Finally we thank Catarina and Julio Jesus and Tim O'Hara for coping with the many hours involved in assembling and reviewing all the contributions, and in compiling this book. The final stage happened in the lovely setting of Oxford, England.

Maria Rosário Partidário
Riki Thérivel
April 1996

List of Acronyms

2010 HST	2010 High Speed train scenario
2010 REF	2010 reference Scenario
2010 FM	2010 Forced Mobility scenario
CEQ	Council on Environmental Quality, US
CEQA	California Environmental Quality Act
CP	comprehensive land-use plan
CSF	Community Support Framework
CTP	Community transport policy
DGVII	Directorate-General for Transport (of the European Commission)
DGXI	Directorate-General of Environment (of the European Commission)
EA	environmental assessment
EARP	Environmental Assessment and Review Process, Canada
EIA	environmental impact assessment
EIR	environmental impact report
EIS	environmental impact statement
ER&WM PEIS	Environmental Restoration and Waste Management Programmatic Environmental Impact Statement
E-test	Environmental Test
EU	European Union
FAERO	Federal Environmental Assessment and Review Office, Canada
FIPA	Farm Income Protection Act, Canada
HSR	High Speed Rail network
IP	Implementation Plan
MPFS	Master Plan for the Forestry Sector, Nepal
NDDB	Natural Diversity Data Base
NEPA	National Environmental Policy Act, 1969
NEPP	National Environmental Policy Plan
NOI	Notice of Intent
NRA	Natural Resources Act, Sweden
NRMA	National Research Management Plan

OFMP	Operational Forest Management Plan, Nepal
PBA	Planning and Building Act, Sweden
PEIS	programmatic EIS
PPG12	Planning Policy Guidance Note 12
PPP	policy, plan or programme
RMA	Resource Management Act, New Zealand
SEA	strategic environmental assessment
SPD	Single Programming Document
TENs	trans-European transport networks
TYP92	Ten-Year Programme on Waste Management 1992–2002
WMC	Waste Management Council, The Netherlands

List of Illustrations

Boxes

Figures

Tables

Part I

Background

1
Introduction

Riki Thérivel and Maria Rosário Partidário

The practical application of strategic environmental assessment (SEA) – the environmental assessment of policies, plans and programmes – has grown by leaps and bounds in the last few years. Whilst very few countries have formal SEA regulations, some have issued guidance on how SEAs should be carried out. Ad hoc SEAs have been carried out in a large number of countries. New SEA regulations and guidelines are being proposed worldwide, including a European SEA directive and national SEA legislations in many European countries. In Australia a major review process of the environmental impact assessment system is under way, including the specific consideration of SEA.

This book shows how SEA has been implemented in practice in the last few years. It aims to give ideas and inspiration to those who are commissioning, carrying out, reviewing, and teaching about SEA. It also aims to promote best practice in SEA. Almost every SEA we have looked at shows elements of good or best practice, but no SEA has included all of these elements. The analyses and case studies presented here should give valuable ideas for how other, future SEAs can be effectively carried out.

Chapters 1 to 3 set the context for the remaining case study chapters. Chapter 2 reviews SEA regulations and guidance worldwide. Chapter 3 discusses SEA models and methodologies. Chapters 4 to 13 are case study chapters. The case studies were collected from countries that have considerable experience with SEA, or where particularly good examples were known to exist. They are organised in three sections: sectoral SEAs, SEAs of land-use plans, and policy SEA. The case studies exemplify different scales, different countries, and different approaches to SEA. The final chapter briefly discusses some issues identified in the case-studies as being constraints to an effective SEA process, as well as positive learning points on how SEA can contribute to the increased effectiveness of environmental assessment.

This chapter reviews what SEA is, who uses it, why it is needed and what some of its limitations are. It then discusses how SEA fits into the decision-making process for policies, plans and programmes, and considers the structure of the case study chapters in more detail.

Definitions

The simple definition of SEA is that it is the environmental assessment (EA) of a strategic action: a policy, plan or programme (PPP). In this sense, SEA should be seen as an EA tool, on a par with other EA tools such as project EIA, cumulative impact assessment and auditing. More specifically, SEA is:

> *the formalised, systematic and comprehensive process of evaluating the environmental effects of a policy, plan or programme and its alternatives, including the preparation of a written report on the findings of that evaluation, and using the findings in publicly accountable decision-making. (Thérivel et al, 1992).*

SEAs therefore differ from:

- environmental impact assessments (EIAs; the term is used in this book only in relation to projects) of large-scale projects because these are site-specific and normally involve only one activity, and are therefore not strategic;
- 'integrated' PPP-making, which incorporates environmental issues in the PPP-making process but does not involve the stages of a formal EA process, particularly an appraisal of alternatives based on environmental objectives and criteria;
- environmental audits or 'state of the environment' reports, which do not predict the future environmental impacts resulting from the application of a PPP;
- SEA studies, which do not influence decision making;
- many 'environmental appraisals', environmental strategies or cost-benefit analyses: those which do not predict the likely future effects of a PPP, do not consider a range of environmental components, and/or do not result in a written report; and
- various integrated management plans which deal with environmental impacts on a specific biotope (eg coast, heathland) but do not specifically inform decision making on alternative planning and development options that could result in sounder environmental outcomes.

SEA is only one of various terms used to refer to EA at the strategic level. Others include policy EA, policy impact assessment, sectoral EAs, programmatic environmental impact statement, EA of PPPs and integration of EA into policy-making. The word 'strategic' in SEA has diverse meanings in the sequence of decisions, from broad policy visions to quite specific programmes of more concrete activities. The function of SEA, and the terminology associated with that function, are still subject to extensive debate. Each country, political or economic system will need to adopt the process and terminology most suitable to that context, in a way that is practical and responsive to integrative approaches towards sustainability goals. It is not the intention of this book to discuss the value of different forms, or definitions, of SEA. The book simply assumes that SEA addresses the strategic component in decision instruments at the policy, planning or programmatic level. The *strategic component* refers to the set of objectives, principles and policies that give shape to the vision and development intentions incorporated in a PPP. SEA deals with concepts, and not with particular activities in terms of their location or technical design (Partidário, 1994).

The difference between *policies, plans* and *programmes* in practice is not very clear. Wood and Djeddour (1992) suggest that:

> *A policy may ... be considered as the inspiration and guidance for action, a plan as a set of co-ordinated and timed objectives for the implementation of the policy, and a programme as a set of projects in a particular area.*

However, in practice this sequence can vary: for instance, in the UK, national level planning policy guidance affects local authority development plans, which in turn are composed of policies and individual site proposals. In Canada, policies directly affect the shaping of programmes, and subsequently individual projects. In Portugal's regional development programmes, programmes of policies provide the context for the development of plans and individual projects at the same level. What is important is that one policy, plan or programme often sets the structure for another PPP, which in turn may influence projects, and thus there is a hierarchy or *tiering* of PPPs. This book mostly uses the generic term 'PPP'. However, where a distinction between tiers needs to be made, it follows the sequence:

policy ⇨ plan ⇨ programme ⇨ project

As PPPs are tiered, so can SEAs be, with higher-level SEAs setting the context for lower-level SEAs, which in turn set the context for project EIAs. Figure 1.1 shows the broad stages of the PPP and SEA processes.

SEA can be applied to three main types of actions: sectoral PPPs, which are related to specific sectors (eg mineral extraction, energy, tourism); area-based or comprehensive PPPs, which cover all activities in a given area (eg land-use or development plans); and actions that do not give rise to projects but nevertheless have a significant environmental impact (eg agricultural practices, new technologies, privatisation). Table 1.1 gives examples of PPPs for which SEAs have been carried out to date.

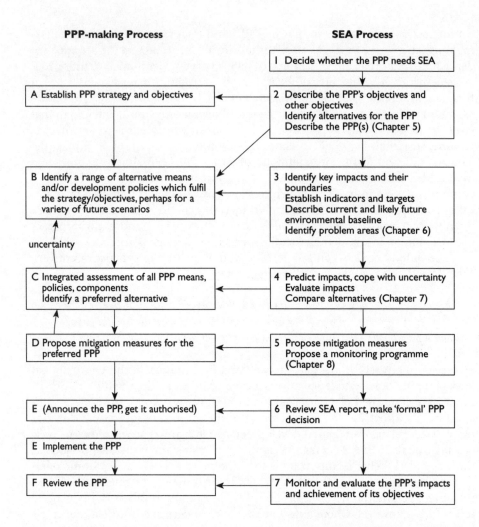

PPP-making Process

SEA Process

1 Decide whether the PPP needs SEA

A Establish PPP strategy and objectives

2 Describe the PPP's objectives and other objectives
Identify alternatives for the PPP
Describe the PPP(s) (Chapter 5)

B Identify a range of alternative means and/or development policies which fulfil the strategy/objectives, perhaps for a variety of future scenarios

3 Identify key impacts and their boundaries
Establish indicators and targets
Describe current and likely future environmental baseline
Identify problem areas (Chapter 6)

uncertainty

C Integrated assessment of all PPP means, policies, components
Identify a preferred alternative

4 Predict impacts, cope with uncertainty
Evaluate impacts
Compare alternatives (Chapter 7)

D Propose mitigation measures for the preferred PPP

5 Propose mitigation measures
Propose a monitoring programme (Chapter 8)

E (Announce the PPP, get it authorised)

6 Review SEA report, make 'formal' PPP decision

E Implement the PPP

F Review the PPP

7 Monitor and evaluate the PPP's impacts and achievement of its objectives

Figure 1.1 *Stages in, and Links Between, PPP-making and SEA*

Interest Groups in SEA

Four main interest groups are involved in SEA: the action-leading agent (proponent), the competent authority, the environmental authority and the public.

The *action-leading agent* is the organisation responsible for developing the PPP. This could be a private company, such as an electricity generating company or the proponent of a new technology; a public sector agency such as the ministry for energy, or a local authority; or a consortium of private and/or public sector organisations, such as a group of housing developers or a regional council composed of several local authorities.

Table 1.1 *Examples of Tiers of SEAs*

Level of government	Land use/Area-based plan	Sectoral and multi-sectoral actions		
		policy	plan	programme
Inter-national/ national	• National development plan 1994–1999 (Portugal)	• Forest Service resource management (US) • Crop insurance (Canada)[13]	• Waste management (Netherlands)[7] • Environmental restoration and waste management (US)[5]	• Nuclear complex reconfiguration (US) • Trans-European rail network (EC)[6] • Chemical stockpile disposal (US)
Regional	• Structural Fund applications for Obj. 1, 2 and 5b regions (EC)[12]		• Windfarm siting in Soest (Germany)[4]	• Cross-Channel Rail Link (UK–France) • Lower Colne River flood alleviation (UK) • Vegetation management in the Ozark/ Ouachita mountains (US) • Forestry strategy (UK)
Local	• Hertford-shire (UK)[9] • Sollentuna (Sweden)[10] • San Joaquin (US)[11]	• Ettrick and Lauderdale sustainable development (Scotland)	• Bara Forest management (Nepal)[8]	• Firth of Forth transport strategy (Scotland) • Columbia River highway (US)

* Numbers in bold relate to the number of the relevant chapter in this book

The *competent authority* – usually a government or quasi-government organisation – is responsible for deciding on the PPP. The action-leading agent and the competent authority are usually the same, public, organisation: for instance a transport ministry could propose a road policy and programme, prepare the

SEA and decide whether the programme should go ahead. This has the disadvantage of potential vested interests and bias, especially where the PPP proponent carries out the SEA and decides whether the PPP should be approved (the 'poacher–gamekeeper syndrome'). However, it has the advantage of allowing the PPP to be more easily refined based on the findings of the SEA.

The *environmental authorit(y)ies* contribute information to, and are consulted as part of, the SEA process. They could include the relevant environment agency, local wildlife groups, and pollution regulatory organisations.

Few SEAs have made a concerted effort to seek and address *public* opinions, for reasons of confidentiality, because the PPP may be considered too sensitive for public debate prior to approval or because of the sheer complexity of consulting the public on a national or region-wide issue. Often the general public does not comment on strategic decisions even where its input is actively sought. As such, the public is often represented by various pressure groups and elected representatives.

Need for SEA

The reasons SEA is needed generally divide into two groups: SEA counteracts some of the limitations of project EIA, and it promotes sustainable development.

Counteracting the Limitations of Project EIA

Although project EIA is becoming widely used and accepted as a useful tool in decision-making, it largely reacts to development proposals rather than proactively anticipating them. Because EIAs take place once many strategic decisions have already been made, they often address only a limited range of alternatives and mitigation measures; those of a wider nature are generally poorly integrated into project planning. Consultation in EIA is limited, and the contribution of EIA to the eventual decision regarding the project is not clear (CEC, 1993; DoE, 1991; Glasson et al, 1995; Lee and Brown, 1992; Thérivel et al, 1992).

Project EIAs are also generally limited to the project's direct impacts. This approach ignores such impacts as:

- the additive effects of many small projects or management schemes that do not require EIA, for instance, agricultural management schemes or defence projects;
- induced impacts, where one project stimulates other development. For instance, the construction of a new road can induce both new traffic (where there is suppressed demand) and new developments such as out-of-town shopping centres or new towns. The EIAs for power stations,

which clearly cannot function without transmission lines, generally do not consider the environmental impacts of these lines (Sheate, 1995);

- synergistic impacts, where the impact of several projects exceeds the mere sum of their individual impacts. For instance, several projects that each encroach on a wildlife site only minimally may, together, affect the site to an extent where it can no longer support certain species; and
- global impacts such as biodiversity and greenhouse gas emissions (Wood, 1995).

SEA can deal with many of these difficulties. It can incorporate environmental issues intrinsically into project planning by influencing the context within which project decisions are made. It allows the consideration of alternatives or mitigation measures that go beyond the confines of individual projects, such as different modes (eg train, bicycle) of getting from A to B, or the creation of wildlife corridors that affect several landowners. It could also allow for consultation on these more strategic issues.

Promoting Sustainable Development

SEA can also play a significant role in enhancing the integration of environmental concerns in policy and planning processes, thereby helping to implement sustainable development. A more integrated system of planning means that environmental and sustainability criteria are incorporated throughout the planning process, for instance, in the identification of suitable (or unsuitable) locations for development, and in the assessment of alternative PPPs. An SEA framework could allow the principle of sustainability to be carried down from policies to individual projects. It could help to ensure that environmental and sustainability considerations are incorporated into the objective of a PPP; it could identify environmental and sustainability benchmarks by which the effects of a PPP can be tested; and it could appraise whether the impacts of a PPP are likely to be in accordance with sustainability objectives.

A new framework for SEA may need to be developed, which could be seen as a new environmental evaluation tool, based primarily on EIA but more efficiently applied to environmentally integrated planning and policy levels. PPP processes could then evolve towards more desirable, sustainable approaches in the future. Figure 1.2 shows how SEA can assist the integration of environmental concerns in PPP processes to help achieve more sustainable PPP practices (Partidário, 1992). This could ultimately result in the framework of a 'sustainability-led' approach to SEA:

1. commitment to the principle of sustainability;
2. determination of carrying capacity;
3. SEA of all relevant tiers of PPPs and their alternatives;
4. EIA of specific projects within the constraints established by SEA; and

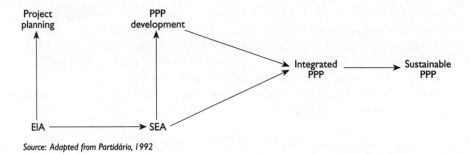

Source: Adapted from Partidário, 1992

Figure 1.2 *SEA: From Project EIA to More Environmental and Sustainable PPP Practices*

5. monitoring and iterative feedback to stages 2–4 (Thérivel et al, 1992; Thompson et al, 1995).

However, the integration of environmental concerns in the PPP should anticipate any SEA. The continuous interaction of multiple factors in policy- and
plan-making means that SEA is truly useful only if environmental concerns have
already been integrated to some extent in the content and approach of the PPP.
Thus SEA and the general integration of environmental considerations in PPP-
making are complementary and mutually reinforcing activities which, together,
can lead to sustainable development.

Limitations of SEA

However SEA also has technical and procedural limitations. On the technical
side, SEAs generally cover a large area – sometimes several countries – and a
large number of alternatives. This makes collecting and analysing data for SEAs
very complex. SEAs are also subject to greater levels of uncertainty than project
EIA: uncertainty about future environmental, economic and social conditions,
uncertainty about the developments likely to take place as a result of the PPP
and uncertainty about likely future technologies. SEAs often have to cope with
limited information where, for instance, environmental data collected in different countries are incompatible or limited. SEAs have to deal with information
at a different level from project EIAs: a national-level SEA needs to focus on
national-level concerns, and thus may have to disregard impacts that are important at a local level but that do not influence a national-level decision. The
relative lack of case studies and experience of SEA exacerbates these limitations: this book aims partially to redress this lack.

   On the procedural side, PPPs are generally nebulous, non-linear, complex
and iterative:

> *Policy ... does not stand still ... it may be inevitable that policy issues are not as precise as many people would wish (House of Commons Environment Committee, 1986).*

This makes it difficult to know when an SEA should be carried out, and what exactly the PPP is that is being assessed. A PPP may have no formal authorisation stage, but instead evolve in fits and starts through to implementation. There may be issues of confidentiality. Decision-makers may also be concerned that SEA should not take over the process of PPP decision-making.

Any SEA system and methodology needs to cope with these issues. SEA must be able to deal with a more nebulous decision-making process, with uncertainty, with larger scales and with induced, secondary and cumulative impacts. The techniques used in SEA are often a combination of those used in traditional policy analysis and those used in EIA. The next section reviews the main models of SEA that are emerging in practice.

SEA in PPP Decision-Making

As will be illustrated in Chapter 2, several general approaches to SEA have evolved, which cope with these issues in different ways:

- The 'consent-related' model is closely related to project EIA. Essentially it adjusts PPP-making where possible to include (a) a formal decision-making stage, and (b) an SEA stage, similar to EIA, which informs the decision-making stage. In Figure 1.1, this model corresponds to the use of SEA primarily at stage E of PPP-making. This model works well for PPPs that already go through an authorisation stage, such as many land-use plans and PPPs for the allocation of funds. Various forms of this model are currently being applied in the US, the UK and the Netherlands.
- The 'integrated' model assumes that PPPs are subject to multiple stages of decision-making (eg choice of objectives, choice of alternatives, choice of mitigation measures), and attempts to integrate SEA into each of these decisions. In Figure 1.1, it corresponds to an emphasis on all the links between the PPP-making and SEA processes. This model essentially relies on a shift in the conceptual approach of decision-makers. This model is broadly promoted in New Zealand and Canada, and by the European Commission.
- The formalisation of the 'integrated' model, supported by a series of regulatory requirements, can evolve into an 'objectives-led' model. This model attempts to readjust PPP-making into a more strategic, transparent and objectives-led process, where SEA sets a framework for subsequent decision-making. This involves (a) establishing sustainability benchmarks

as a main objective which is then 'trickled down' through the various tiers of PPPs, (b) establishing clear top-down links from policies to plans to programmes and (c) identifying clear decision-making stages for each of these PPP tiers. In Figure 1.1, this model corresponds to a formalisation of the PPP-making process, and an emphasis on stage A. The 'objectives-led' model represents a rather utopian situation not yet seen in practice.

In practice, due to the limited application of SEA to date, it is not yet clear whether the different models lead to the use of different SEA techniques and methodologies. SEAs in the US tend to be very comprehensive (and correspondingly bulky), and emphasise public consultation; Dutch SEAs seem to deal particularly well with hierarchies of decision-making; German SEAs seem to emphasise quantification and the use of geographical information systems (GIS); and British SEAs seem to be more qualitative and slimmer. However, these differences may be due to a wide range of factors other than the SEA model and regulatory system. SEA methodologies are discussed further in Chapter 3.

Framework for, and Overview of, the Case Studies

The main emphasis of this book is on case studies. SEA regulations and guidelines (Chapter 2) have been established in only a limited number of countries. SEA methods (Chapter 3) are evolving rapidly, but a clear framework of best practice methods has not yet emerged. At the moment, SEA is primarily progressing through individual case-studies. These, in turn, are leading to a greater understanding of possible SEA methods. Once these become more accepted and widespread, more SEA regulations and guidelines are likely to be established.

Chapters 4 to 13 each address a different case study. The aim of these chapters is to illustrate not only the different scales and types of SEAs but also the methodological approaches used in different national and PPP decision-making contexts. In order to ensure that the same kind of information was included in each chapter and to facilitate the final comparison of these examples, a framework was developed that contributors could use as a term of reference when developing their case studies; this is shown in Table 1.2.

Sectoral SEAs

Chapter 4 discusses the use of SEA in Germany, focusing on its application in the Soest district for siting windfarms. It is a good example of how GIS techniques can help to identify environmentally robust sites for development. It also shows that even PPPs that are broadly environmentally beneficial can still profit from the application of SEA.

Table 1.2 *Framework for the Preparation of Case Studies on SEA Practice*

The action
Type, subject, sector, scale etc
Reason for proposed action
Level of decision-making
Confidentiality
Relevant dates
Proponent, competent authority, other interested groups involved

SEA process: context
Legal and procedural context: volunteered v. required, by whom etc
Guidelines and regulations used, if any
Links to other policies, actions, and projects
Screening process and criteria

SEA process: steps
Who prepared the SEA?
Objectives of the action
Links to sustainable development and carrying capacity
Identification and scoping of impacts
Baseline information
Alternatives considered
Consultation (statutory consultees, public): procedures, results, use of results
Methods used
Mitigation
Review of SEA
Presentation of results: form, length of report etc

Results/effectiveness of SEA
Influence in the final decision
Changes made to the proposed action as a result of the SEA
Effects of the SEA on the timing of the action
Results of monitoring, if any

Conclusions
Recommendations on how to improve SEA process, usefulness of SEA etc

---

Chapter 5 reviews the SEA for a national-level environmental restoration and waste management programme in the US. It is a good example of the consideration of alternatives and the use of public participation in SEA.

Chapter 6 concerns the SEA for the trans-European rail network, a large-scale rail network covering several countries. The SEA analyses a range of future scenarios, and highlights the problems of collecting and analysing incompatible data from different sources.

Chapter 7 discusses the SEA for the Dutch national waste management programme. The use of scenarios and alternatives is particularly interesting, as are the links between the national and regional levels of programme planning.

Chapter 8 considers the SEA for the Bara Forest management plan in Nepal. It is unusual in that it involves SEA in a developing country, and it deals particularly well with socioeconomic issues such as the plan's distributional effects.

SEAs of Comprehensive (Area-Based) Land-Use Plans

Chapter 9 considers SEA in land-use planning in the United Kingdom. It shows how sustainability can be promoted through the use of SEA, and is a good example of how a wide range of interest groups can be involved in SEA.

Chapter 10 analyses the interaction between SEA and municipal land-use planning in Sweden. It focuses on the dialogue between the different interest groups involved, and how choices were made between alternatives.

Chapter 11 discusses the SEA for a draft comprehensive plan in California (US) that used a particularly clear methodology. The case study focuses on the links between the SEA and the plan decision-making process.

Policy SEAs

Chapter 12 considers how the allocation of structure funds – funds for the economic development of Europe's poorer regions – has been made subject to SEA. It discusses the SEA of the Irish structure fund application, and changes made to the funding proposal as a result of the SEA.

Chapter 13 discusses a follow-up SEA for Canada's crop insurance policy, which involves financial protection against the effect of natural hazards on cultivated crops. It discusses the trade-offs between physical, social and economic issues in SEA particularly well.

The final chapter highlights the issues arising from these case studies, and identifies some likely future trends in SEA.

2
SEA Regulations and Guidelines Worldwide

Maria Rosário Partidário

Introduction

Examples of regulatory systems of SEA are still relatively scarce. With a very few exceptions (eg New Zealand, the Netherlands and the US), most countries in which SEA has been carried out in practice do not yet have a legislated process. Experience with SEA is emerging, essentially based on self-learning case studies that focus on particular types of comprehensive (area-wide) and sectoral PPP activities.

The development of SEA is showing similar trends to that of project EIA during the 1970s. Attention is primarily focused on understanding SEA as a concept; on its scope and range of application as an environmental assessment tool that, above all, aims to strengthen the principles of EA as currently applied to project EIAs; and on extending these principles to PPPs. In this learning curve, initiatives undertaken reflect the existing experience with project EIAs and the efforts being made towards the development of methodologies and identification of relevant issues that are specific to SEA. Understanding the application of SEA in practical case studies helps to collect the necessary empirical evidence and test scientific findings and assumptions. Translation into appropriate regulations and institutional mechanisms can hence be looked upon as a follow-up step.

Issues of open and democratic economic and political structures also strongly influence the rate at which SEA systems are being, or will be, implemented. For example, in political systems that rely on closed and non-participatory traditions, it is hard to conceive of cabinet decisions or government departments' legislative proposals being open to public scrutiny, as part of the assessment of their environmental effects. However, the fact is that the EA of policy options and planning strategies requires a high degree of openness and flexibility in political attitudes. New initiatives in policy-making and planning must be easily adjustable to rapidly changing priorities in physical, social and economic environments. It is therefore not surprising to see that it is in countries with well-established pluralistic and democratic structures that SEA is evolving more rapidly.

This chapter focuses on current (late 1995) institutional and procedural approaches to SEA in countries where significant contributions already exist. Particular emphasis is placed on regulations and guidelines, since they reflect the institutional frameworks adopted as well as linkages between EA, planning and policy-making provisions, and decision-making processes. The intention is to offer a brief overview of emerging SEA systems and associated mechanisms, thus providing relevant references for those intending to adopt similar processes in particular national contexts. The countries reviewed include Canada, the US, the Netherlands, the UK, Denmark, Sweden, Norway, Finland, Germany, France, New Zealand and Australia. The status of SEA in international organisations such as the World Bank and the European Union is also considered. A brief synopsis on the rationale and approaches generally adopted, and challenges and barriers faced in the countries/institutions reviewed, precedes profiles of individual countries.

Evolving Approaches

Rationale

Most countries relate SEA to sustainability goals, on the grounds that SEA may assist the decision-making process by influencing the design of more sustainable policies and strategies. In some cases sustainability remains an implicit background policy (eg in the US, Sweden, Norway, Finland, France, Germany and the UK). In other cases sustainability issues are used as benchmarks against which objectives and criteria in SEA can be measured (eg Canada, the Netherlands, Denmark), or as a strong policy that helps to shape new forms of decision-making in support of sustainable development (eg Australia, New Zealand).

SEA is also related to the consideration of cumulative effects. It is seen as providing a context and rationale within which to address cumulative effects such as the long-term effects that result from the development of a tourist resort, which are not normally addressed on a project-by-project basis. Recent studies developed as part of the Australian review process (Australia, Commonwealth EPA, 1994) highlight the advantages of this relationship between SEA and assessment of cumulative effects. However, evidence for how this synergism is achieved has yet to be demonstrated with adequate methodologies and empirical examples.

SEA is emerging in the context of national environmental policies. In countries where there is longer-standing and/or more extensive experience with project EIA, SEA is seen as an extension of existing EA practices to higher levels of decision-making (eg the US, the Netherlands). Where regional and local planning practices have dominated the environmental policy arena, SEA is more often incorporated within planning practices. This is certainly the case in Nordic countries (eg Denmark, Sweden, Norway, Finland) and also in the UK, France and Germany. Australia and New Zealand have opted for an overall reform of the environmental administrative process. Whilst in New Zealand this process is legally and administratively under way, with the proclamation in 1991 of the Resource Management Act, the Commonwealth of Australia has only more recently undertaken a major review of its EIA process. The option in Canada seems to be the adoption of distinct processes for project EIA and policy impact assessment, with the first now legally enacted and the second issued as a non-legislated process.

From Project EIA to SEA

The extension of project EIA principles to the policy and planning levels has been encountering some resistance and concern amongst policy-makers and planning practitioners. Particularly in the realm of physical planning, practitioners from many countries (eg Sweden, Australia, Denmark) claim that plans already cover project EIA requirements and use similar methodologies such as scope of analysis (natural, social and economic issues), comparison of alternative solutions and conflict–resolution approaches. Applying specific EA mechanisms, such as SEA, to plans and policies would hence be superfluous. However it was in Sweden, where planning provides the context and mechanisms for project EIA to enter the decision-making process, that critical differences between project EIA and planning were identified, thus underlining the particular role of EA at policy and planning levels (Lerman, 1995):

- Development steps are more clear and transparent in project EA and more implicit in planning.
- The disciplines involved in an EA team are often more varied than in a planning team, and public consultation has been more effective.
- Project EIA 'shows' impacts before a decision is reached, thus informing the decision. The plan-making process is often synonymous with the decision-making process. The plan may specify and explain the choices made and the changes foreseen, but this is not its main aim. A specific tool is therefore required to assist in identifying the plan's expected impacts.

- Project EIA uses the no-action alternative to show changes and impacts which would occur in the absence of the proposed project: this is often used to justify the project. Plans generally do not consider a no-action alternative, and thus do not predict what the future would be if the plan was not implemented.

The argument that SEA can improve and facilitate the EIA of site-specific projects has been used to support SEA since its early days. While this relationship is not always obvious, as most countries still neglect to put in place the mechanisms that will ensure it, in some countries it is being suggested that, as a consequence of SEA, more sound and environmentally sensitive policies and plans will incorporate the necessary requirements for the subsequent development of projects (eg the Netherlands, New Zealand, Denmark, the UK). Goodland and Tillman (1995) compare traditional reactive EA and strategic proactive EA, arguing that 'traditional reactive project level EIA is necessary but not sufficient to exploit opportunities which exist today but which may be gone tomorrow', whereas 'SEA improves investments over the long term and should be fed by long term projections'.

Two distinct approaches are being used to apply project EIA to strategic decisions. The first is literally an extension of the practice of project EIA, and applies not only its principles but also the legal procedures and requirements related to the screening and scoping stages, the presentation of environmental impact statements (EISs), the information to be included, predictions, comparison of alternatives and mitigative measures (project-based approach); the second adopts a policy and planning rationale, whereby project EIA principles are tailored in the formulation of policies and plans, through the identification of needs and options for development which are then assessed in the context of a vision for sustainable development (policy-based approach).

Challenges and Barriers

Different countries face a range of challenges and barriers regarding their particular political and institutional contexts for the implementation of SEA. In most cases, however, difficulties seem to derive from the uncertainty and vagueness associated with SEA, and from its potential role in environmental decision-making. Problems felt include a lack of guidance and training, lack of clear accountability and responsibility, lack of resources and unknown or untested methodologies. Table 2.1 summarizes the most often indicated barriers, as reviewed in various papers that critically address the implementation of SEA in national contexts (Partidário, 1994).

Table 2.1 *Barriers to Implementing SEA*

- Lack of knowledge and experience concerning which environmental factors to consider, what environmental impacts might arise and how integrated policy-making can be achieved
- Institutional and organisational difficulties – need for effective coordination amongst and within government departments
- Lack of resources (information, expertise, financial)
- Lack of guidelines or mechanisms to ensure full implementation
- Insufficient political will and commitment to implement SEA
- Difficulty in stating clear policy proposals and in defining when and how SEA should be applied
- Methodologies not well developed
- Limited public involvement
- Lack of clear accountability in the application of the SEA process
- Current project-specific EIA practices are not necessarily applicable to SEA and are inhibiting sound SEA approaches

---

Most Significant Contributions to SEA Regulations and Guidelines

This section highlights different countries' experiences with, and approaches to, SEA. Only countries that have contributed significantly to the development of SEA are referred to. For Canada, the US and Australia only the federal experience will be reviewed. Table 2.2 offers a quick reference to where regulations and guidelines exist. Finland, Germany and France are mentioned in Table 2.2 because of their interest in, and efforts towards, the establishment of an SEA system. However, because of the absence of specific regulations and guidelines, this chapter does not cover the current status of SEA in these countries.

Canada

In federal Canada the application of EA principles to policy and programme decision-making has been ongoing since the late 1980s. Extensive research and numerous discussions conducted in national, bilateral and international workshops contributed to the definition of organisational and procedural mechanisms and the identification of issues and barriers (Bregha et al, 1990; Bridgewater, 1989; Canada, FEARO, 1989 and 1992; Holtz, 1991; Scott, 1992). However, implementation of the federal policy EA requirements is still limited.

SEA is evolving in Canada on various fronts:

Table 2.2 *Current Status of SEA Regulations and Guidelines in Countries Reviewed*

	Application	Regulations	Guidance
US (federal)	Programmes Plans	Provisions for SEA included in the NEPA, 1970	CEQ Guidelines also apply
The Netherlands	Programmes Plans Policies	1987 EIA regulations require SEA for activities in the positive list	No specific guidance for SEA; practice is based on traditional project EIA procedures
	Cabinet decisions	Proposal for an environmental paragraph under discussion	Proposal for an 'E-test' based on checklists and sustainable development criteria
New Zealand	Programmes Plans Policies	Provisions for SEA under the RMA, 1991, and EPEP, 1974	Non-statutory guidance issued by the Ministry of Environment
Denmark	Programmes Plans Bills and other government proposals	No formal regulations Administrative order of 1993	Guidance issued in 1993
Canada (federal)	Policies and programmes to cabinet	Cabinet directive of June 1990	Guidance under preparation
The UK	Programmes Plans Policies	No formal regulations	Guidance issued in 1991 and 1993
Australia (federal)	Programmes Plans Policies	No formal regulations; review process under way	No specific guidance
Sweden	Programmes Plans Policies	No formal regulations; provisions in the planning and natural resources legislation	No specific guidance

Table 2.2 *Continued*

	Application	Regulations	Guidance
Finland	Programmes Plans Policies	No formal regulations	No specific guidance
Germany	Programmes Plans Policies	No formal regulations	No specific guidance
France	Programmes Plans Policies	No formal regulations	No specific guidance

NEPA: National Environmental Policy Act; CEQ: Council on Environmental Quality; EPEP: Environmental Protection and Enhancement Procedures; E-test: environmental test; RMA: Resource Management Act.

- as part of a strong commitment to integrate environmental and economic issues into a national strategy for sustainable development (Canada, Projet de Société, 1994);
- through the development of integrated approaches to resource planning and management (eg integrated resource management plans) that also seek to consider related cumulative effects; and
- as a new government requirement first announced as part of the federal government's reform of the Environmental Assessment and Review Process (EARP) in 1990.

A cabinet directive issued in 1990 requires all federal departments and agencies to apply a mandatory, yet non-legislated, environmental process to federal policy and programme proposals submitted for cabinet consideration, that are likely to have environmental impacts. Its purpose is to ensure a systematic integration of environmental considerations into the planning and decision-making processes, so that information about the environmental implications of proposals can support decision-making in the same way economic, social and cultural factors do. In 1993 the Federal Environmental Assessment and Review Office released a document outlining the procedural requirements of the cabinet directive (Canada, FEARO, 1993). This includes a generic, non-prescriptive procedure, which allows for much discretion in applying policy EA. The decision on the relevance of environmental impacts is left to the discretion of the minister submitting the proposal (Canada, FEARO, 1993). Whilst the scope of coverage is quite clear, methodological, substantive and procedural aspects lack specific definition (Canada, FEARO, 1994).

In order to meet the requirements for policy EA, a few federal departments and agencies have developed specific internal procedures and guidelines to assist the implementation of the 1990 directive, underlining the need to make EA an inherent component of policy and decision-making processes (CIDA, 1993; NRCan, 1993; Canada, DOE, 1994; Canada, EMR, 1994). Approaches proposed range from rather non-specific elements to be attached to a policy proposal (eg reasoned written letter and environmental communiqué, with specification of contexts left to the discretion of managers) (Canada, EMR, 1994), to more thorough processes that identify the sequence of assessment and review stages and information requirements (NRCan, 1993; Canada, DOE, 1994). Chapter 13 gives an example of a more comprehensive SEA approach. A guide for policy EA is under development within the Canadian Environmental Assessment Agency, in consultation with federal departments (LeBlanc, 1994).

The new Canadian Environmental Assessment Act of January 1995 applies only to project EIAs. This certainly reflects a feeling that policy and programme EA, or SEA, though acknowledging the same principles, must be treated in a form that differs from the requirements for project EIA.

The US

Programmatic EISs (PEISs) represent the main SEA approach in the US. Most PEISs essentially involve groups of projects that have technical or geographical similarities, and thus result in a site-specific analysis. Whether this represents a form of SEA is arguable. The National Environmental Policy Act (NEPA) of 1969 provides the legal context for PEISs, and Council on Environmental Quality (CEQ) regulations give guidance on how the act should be implemented. There are no federal guidelines which apply specifically to SEA. Some key barriers SEA practitioners face in the US include a piecemeal approach to PEISs, multiple decision-making processes compounded by a lack of coordination within and amongst the various agencies, and a process that is fundamentally product oriented (production of an EIS).

Nevertheless, some PEISs address policy options in a broader sense, so that an analysis of the policy concept is carried out, and options are identified and released for public consultation, stating the advantages and disadvantages of adopting each option in an EA. This has been undertaken by the US Department of Energy in a few cases. Technological assessment is also indicated in the US as a form of SEA, since it questions the environmental effects of adopting a range of alternative technologies for a specific purpose.

Ecosystem-based planning approaches have been evolving in the past few years and may provide a planning context for SEA. The recently issued Government Performance and Results Act, which aims at increasing government budget and resource efficiency, requires agencies to prepare five-year strategic plans and report to Congress on an annual basis. Although there are no requirements in terms of EA, environmental strategic instruments that incorporate vision statements are being prepared in this context by some federal agencies (US Bureau of Land Management, National Oceanic and Atmospheric Administration, Parks Service).

The Netherlands

SEA evolved in the context of a national strategy and framework action plan, the National Environmental Policy Plan (NEPP), aimed at achieving sustainable development (Netherlands, MHPPE, 1989 and 1990). Two concurrent SEA systems appear to be evolving. The first is driven by the existing EIA regulatory framework, based on the 1987 Environmental Protection (General Provisions) Act, which covers certain types of plans and programmes (see Table 2.3). Chapter 7 gives an example of an SEA for the Dutch national waste management programme carried out under this system.

The second system, responding to a cabinet decision on the extension of EIA requirements to policy proposals, calls for an 'Environmental Test', or 'E-test', to be used where EIA, according to the act, does not apply. Policy proposals should contain an EA paragraph that details the estimated effects of the policy on the environment; this will have equal weight to the economic assessment paragraph currently prepared for all policy proposals (Dutch Environmental Policy Action no 6). The proposed procedure is based on a step-by-step approach and a checklist of sustainability criteria which are used to assess policy areas (Netherlands, Directorate for General Policy Affairs, 1992). It is the responsibility of each ministry, in each policy area, to conduct and apply the E-test, whilst overall coordination is the responsibility of the Ministry of the Environment (Netherlands, ACET, 1993).

According to the NEPP action point A141, the relationship between government policies and sustainable development must be determined. Using the E-test, each ministry will report on how its policy and associated set of instru-

Table 2.3 *Plans and Programmes Covered by the Dutch Environmental Protection (General Provisions) Act*

- Structural schemes for land development
- Land development plans (or modification of these plans)
- Plans for industrial processes and drinking water supply
- Plans concerning the methods, facilities for or locations of waste disposal
- Plans for the use of fuels, fissile materials or wind energy in existing and planned electric power stations and other installations for generating electricity
- Decrees by which the designation of nature reserves is rescinded
- All national physical plans fixing the location(s) of projects mentioned in the EIA decree

ments will meet the objectives of sustainable development. A methodology was developed to assist this requirement, whereby the instruments' positive or inhibiting effects on sustainable development are analysed and a summary is presented. The experience gained in this process will be of great benefit to the adoption, implementation and improvement of the E-test and pragmatic use of an environmental paragraph, which synthesizes the key environmental impacts resulting from policy implementation (as required under NEPP action point A142) (Netherlands, Directorate for General Policy Affairs, 1992).

The UK

In the UK, two distinct approaches to SEA are evolving: so-called 'environmental appraisals' of (1) government policies and (2) local authority development plans. Government policies are primarily appraised through an extended form of economic analysis. Environmental appraisal of development plans adopts a more physical approach, integrating biophysical, social and economic issues in plan formulation and decision-making, based on a combination of planning and project EIA principles and methodologies.

The rationale for undertaking SEA in the UK, at both policy and development plan levels, is founded on sustainability issues (UK Cabinet, 1994) and on a longer tradition of economic appraisal, such as the application of compliance cost assessment to evaluate costs to businesses of complying with regulations. SEA of UK policies and plans aims to achieve six objectives (UK DoE, 1991):

- systematic analysis of costs and benefits associated with a particular policy;
- exploration of the economic implications of environmental policies;
- exploration of the environmental implications of economic policies;
- exploration of the relative cost-effectiveness of different means of delivering environmental policies;
- internalisation of environmental externalities; and
- improvement of procedures for appraising costs and benefits in particular policy areas.

The government's advice on policy appraisal applies across a wide range of government policies and programmes, not just those with direct environmental aims. Institutional integration is advised in the guidance to ensure integrated decision-making. For policy appraisal, a cost–benefit approach to alternatives is suggested, including discounting techniques that evaluate benefits now and in the future. However, ethical issues and societal values are not considered, which presents difficulties in monetary valuation (UK DoE, 1991, 1994).

Many development plans in the UK are now being appraised (see Chapter 9 for an example), and increasingly British government environmental appraisal guidance is being applied (UK DoE, 1993). This includes identification of key environmental issues and preparation of scoping frameworks and multisectoral matrices to assess (1) the compatibility of the plan with national government environmental guidance; (2) the internal compatibility of the plan strategy and policies; and (3) the plan's impact on the environment. This approach is believed to be of value in introducing the best environmental practice in the planning process. In so doing, the application of SEA to policies and plans provides a tiered approach to project EIAs.

Difficulties encountered in SEA in Britain relate essentially to problems in applying cost-benefit analysis. One of the challenges in the UK sustainable development policy is to find mechanisms that will assess how people value environmental resources.

Denmark

EA concerns are rooted in long-standing environmental planning practice. Project EIA began as a simple extension of existing planning legislation. However, the need for a gradual integration of EA principles and procedures in the decision-making process was recognised by the Danish government. New mechanisms for the introduction of SEA are being put in place to address government proposals (bills, statements etc), but not plans and programmes. Government environmental and sustainable development action plans, developed since 1987, provide environmental objectives which act as a relevant framework for the assessment of government proposals (Denmark, Ministry of the Environment, 1994).

SEA in Denmark is required under an administrative order and not by law. In 1993 the prime minister issued a cabinet circular on commercial and environmental impacts which calls for SEA of all government proposals with major environmental effects. The process is discretionary, and SEA is to be carried out by the appropriate ministries only if significant environmental impacts are likely to occur. In order to assist individual ministers, a guide was issued by the Ministry of the Environment, which provides advice and guidance on how to carry out assessments on a qualitative basis, supported by a collection of SEA studies as examples of application (Denmark, Ministry of the Environment, 1994). A screening checklist is used in the guide to identify impacts and their importance. Impacts on physical, ecological, cultural, health and risk factors are to be assessed. The assessment also addresses cumulative impacts, such as multiple minor impacts (Denmark, Ministry of the Environment, 1994; Elling, 1994).

Sweden

As in Denmark, EA in Sweden evolved in the context of the planning system. This seems to be a common approach in Nordic countries, whereby the plan-

ning and EA rationale share common principles and decision-making mechanisms. In Sweden, the planning system, the natural resources management
system and EIA are closely linked. The Natural Resource Management Act
(NRA) of 1987 provides a common basis for decisions which involve changing
land use, providing the rules and setting the borders. There are requirements to
address the public interest as part of the planning and resource management
process. The description of the public interest is found in municipality-wide comprehensive plans, which are regulated under the Planning and Building Act (PBA)
(Balfors, 1994; Lerman, 1994).

The approach to SEA in Sweden is based on the need to support the application of planning and natural resource management regulations and to assess
the effects of choices being made at that level. All NRA-related decisions must
take into account long-term changes on the ecological, social and economic
environment. An environmental impact statement is required within the NRA
and the PBA, as part of the activity-permitting process, whenever there is any
change of land use. The EIS must address the impacts of the land-use change
on human health, the environment and the management of resources. The environment refers to the surroundings such as land, air, water, animals and plants
as well as landscape and cultural values. There are no further SEA process regulations or guidance provided. The purpose, however, is not to make SEA into
something separate from planning, or to create separate procedures, but to integrate SEA into physical planning, as a supplementary tool.

Alternatives are to be considered, including the no-action alternative. No
requirements exist in terms of content of the EIS, which is left to the discretion
of the proponent. The preparation of the EIS is motivated by a need to provide
information for the application of the NRA, to widen the scope of factors considered and to address cumulative and synergistic impacts. A major challenge,
however, is the need to improve the quality of the NRA-system with new regulations. According to Lerman (1994), the process needs to be more transparent,
to promote critical review, and to require decisions to be justified. Chapter 10
gives two examples of the integration of SEA in land-use planning in Sweden.

New Zealand

In New Zealand, application of EA at policy level is variable in a system which
is devolved, flexible and not prescriptive (Dixon and Fookes, 1995). The
Resource Management Act (RMA) provides for the integration of project EIA
within the planning system as a broader process of environmental assessment.
EA, planning, decision-making and monitoring are linked in a systematic
approach to resource management, so that the assessment of environmental
effects in the context of sustainable management forms the cornerstone of the
RMA (Dixon, 1993; Dixon and Fookes, 1995).

The act is administered by 12 regional councils and 74 district and city
councils. It focuses primarily on the management of physical and natural

resources, with the intention that economic activity is sustainable in a physical and ecological sense (Dixon, 1994). Under the RMA, policy statements and plans provide the policies and rules which govern local administration of resource consents covering land activities, land subdivision, water use permits, discharge permits and coastal activities (Dixon and Fookes, 1995). One innovative feature of the RMA is the provision for EA of policies and plans prepared by local government.

Section 32 of the act requires that policies and plans adopted by local government be accompanied by an analysis of the implications for achieving sustainable management of the environment (Dixon, 1993). The RMA requires councils to review:

- the extent to which any objective, rule, policy or other method is necessary in achieving the purpose of the act;
- other means of achieving the same end;
- the reasons for and against adopting the policy or mechanism and the principal alternatives, including doing nothing; and
- the likely benefits and costs of the principal alternatives (Veart, 1994).

Local government must also explicitly monitor the effectiveness of its decision-making tools (eg consent compliance), as well as policy outcomes, and adopt state-of-the environment reporting. Consultation is a strong feature of the RMA, with specific provisions for pre-hearing meetings, dispute resolution and mediation.

In New Zealand there is a sound legislative framework for project EIAs, but it is more implicit at the policy level. Tools and techniques to meet the challenge are lacking, especially at the policy- and plan-making level of resource management (Veart, 1994; Ward, 1994). For example, councils are not required to produce specific EAs of policies and plans. The RMA does not dictate how policy statements and plans should be constructed, although non-statutory guidelines were prepared (Dixon and Fookes, 1995). However, many practitioners thought these were inadequate to assist with a major shift in approach from the traditional land-use plans prepared under former legislation to resource management plans based more on effects.

The need to set parameters and indicators which incorporate risk and uncertainty to achieve benchmarks against which environmental impacts can be assessed is another challenge posed by the implementation of SEA in New Zealand.

Australia

In federal Australia, cabinet documents concerning significant economic, environmental and social issues that have the potential to affect ecological processes must be assessed in terms of the implications of their recommendations and conclusions on the National Strategy for Ecologically Sustainable Development. This assessment must include economic, environmental and social impacts. This is part of the government's commitment to incorporate ecologically sustainable development principles into decision-making (Australia, Cabinet, 1994). A key principle is that it will be necessary to change the way decisions are made if the objectives of ecologically sustainable development are to be met. Adoption of SEA is intended to ensure that policy-making takes account of sustainability principles.

Current legislation on environmental protection does not take account of SEA, and there is no mechanism for its incorporation. However, SEA has a role to play as a policy-making tool: it should have regard for cumulative, regional and long-term impacts, and should evaluate development proposals in a carrying capacity context. SEA and cumulative impact assessment are viewed as being closely aligned in the review materials of the Commonwealth Government EIA process (Australia, Commonwealth EPA, 1994).

European Union

The adoption of a specific directive that would address the environmental impacts of PPPs has been under discussion in the European Union for several years. The first draft of this directive was already being debated in the late 1980s. However, in 1990 it was considered inappropriate to initiate such a new EA process, since it was felt to be more important that member states concentrate their efforts on the review of the five-year implementation of the project EIA directive. In 1995 this discussion was re-initiated, and a draft directive is currently being reviewed by member states for comments and suggestions. There is, however, much uncertainty about when the new directive on EA of plans and programmes (probably not policies) will finally be implemented.

An SEA procedure is internally in operation within the Commission. In 1993 an internal communication was adopted by the Commission addressing all future Commission strategic actions as well as new legislative proposals likely to have significant impacts on the environment. Under these procedures all directorates-general may now be made responsible for the environmental consequences of their initiatives. In response, all structural fund applications now need to be accompanied by a form of SEA; this is discussed further in Chapter 12. The Habitats Directive (92/43) also includes a requirement for SEA of plans affecting special areas of conservation or special protection areas.

The European Commission's interest in SEA is also reflected in the various research projects that have been commissioned in the last few years (European Commission, 1994). Recent SEA research projects and initiatives are no longer restricted to the directorate-general responsible for the environment, but cut across all sectors of activity within the Commission. Chapter 6 gives an example of this.

World Bank

In 1989, in the context of the greening of its business policy, the World Bank adopted Operational Directive 4.00, which requires SEA to be applied to regional and sectoral development activities. Although this form of SEA clearly evolved from a project EIA perspective, the fact that it was being applied to a new range of strategic activities was a significant step forward in SEA.

Regional EAs were used where a number of development activities, with potential cumulative impacts, were planned for a certain area. These regional EAs were quite heavily influenced by existing US programmatic environmental impact statements. Sectoral EAs, however, had a much more strategic character and were considered adequate for use in the design of sectoral investment programmes. The Environmental Assessment Sourcebook (World Bank, 1991) contains a set of sectoral guidelines that apply to regional and sectoral EAs.

The World Bank experience with respect to the application of regional and particularly sectoral EAs is extensive (World Bank, 1993 and 1994). The intention has been to include sectoral EAs as part of the routine of sectoral studies, providing planners with the most environmentally and economically sound strategy for meeting development objectives according to established priorities. Although perhaps not so much part of the routine as ideally they should be, the variety of situations and development actions to which sectoral EAs have been applied is demonstrative of their utility (Goodland and Tillman, 1995).

Within the Bank's experience regarding SEA, privatisation and structural adjustment operations are amongst the Bank's most important activities in the last few years. This forms an important addition to the range of actions and activities to which SEAs are applicable.

Conclusions

Table 2.2 presents a synopsis of the descriptions offered in this chapter. The list of references facilitates the identification of further reading for those interested in particular types of approaches to SEA.

The situation regarding existing regulations for SEA and the adoption of specific guidance is quite variable. In particular, the existence of guidelines and regulations does not guarantee effective use of SEA in practice, nor does the absence of formal SEA regulations prevent SEA practice. Many of the SEA case studies presented in subsequent chapters were carried out in the absence of SEA regulations. However, it is likely, on the basis of existing practical experience, as shown in some of the case studies, that new regulations and guidelines will be established in the future.

3

SEA Methodology in Practice

Riki Thérivel

This chapter discusses how SEA methodologies – the approaches and techniques used to carry out SEAs – are used in practice, based on an analysis of approximately 100 SEAs from around the world. It shows that, contrary to popular belief, SEA techniques do exist and are usable in their present form. This chapter is structured according to the sequence of SEA stages shown in Figure 1.1. Although the stages will be discussed individually, they are – or should be – inextricably interlinked, with feedback loops as shown in the figure. Not every SEA will involve all of the stages, nor will all the stages be carried out in the same depth. Similarly, not all of the methodologies are useful for all types of SEAs. Box 3.1 identifies key considerations that affect what methodologies are used for a given SEA.

The methodologies discussed here broadly reflect an 'integrated' SEA model, as this seems to be the current best practice. In particular, this model involves identifying the policy plan or programme's sustainability or environmental objectives; linking these objectives to indicators; and using the indicators to test the attainment of the objectives, describe the baseline environment, make impact predictions, and monitor the effect, and effectiveness, of the PPP.

This chapter does not distinguish between different tiers of PPP (eg policy vs programme), nor between different SEA models, primarily because there are not enough examples of the application of each tier and model to allow a clear distinction to be drawn, but also because most elements of good practice SEA are applicable to most tiers and models of SEA.

Setting Objectives and Targets

Every PPP has a purpose, which can be stated as one or several objectives. For

---

Box 3.1 *Key Considerations in Choosing SEA Techniques*

1. Will this technique or approach help achieve the objectives of this step of the process? What is the best technique at this stage for:
   - identifying linkages?
   - estimating and forecasting effects and consequences?
   - assessing significance?
2. Does the magnitude and potential significance of the impacts warrant the level of effort required by the technique?
   - cost?
   - timing?
   - involvement of key personnel?
   - involvement of peers, outside experts and public stakeholders?
3. Is it possible and practical to utilise techniques under consideration?
   - are peers, experts and stakeholders available and willing to participate?
   - do adequate and reliable data exist?
4. Are there any other factors that may influence selection of approaches and techniques?
   - strictures of confidentiality?
   - skill levels and capacity to design and implement given techniques?
   - personal preferences of parties involved?

Source: FEARO, 1995

---

some PPPs, these objectives may be explicitly and easily identified, whilst for others they are implicit, being the result of a large number of small incremental decisions made as part of the political process. However, even when the PPP is unstated, objectives are nevertheless there. Without a clear idea of a PPP's objectives, it is impossible to ensure that the PPP achieves those objectives, to test whether the PPP's objectives are in line with those of higher-level PPPs, or to implement the PPP effectively.

A PPP may have a hierarchy of objectives. Generally a PPP's primary objectives will involve a balance of economic, social and environmental priorities, and can only be stated very vaguely. An example for an energy policy might be 'to satisfy country X's energy requirements at minimal economic and environmental cost'. In turn, the primary objective could lead to more specific objectives, such as reducing energy consumption, promoting diversified sources of energy and protecting the physical and cultural environment. This can lead to more precise environmental objectives which can be used in SEA, for instance 'to minimise emissions of nitrogen oxides'.

Obviously, objectives of some PPPs are primarily environmental, such as those of policies for preserving particularly sensitive landscape or ecological areas. Others, like privatisation or deregulation, are primarily economic. However, most PPPs will have a mixture of objectives, some of which may not be mutually compatible. SEAs do not themselves draw the balance between these priorities; that is a political process to which SEA merely contributes information.

Objectives may involve a direction of change, for instance 'to increase the area covered by designated wildlife sites in region X' or 'to reduce carbon dioxide emissions'. Alternatively, they can set quantified targets or benchmarks to be achieved by a certain date, for instance 'to increase the area covered by designated wildlife sites in region X by 10 percent' or 'to reduce carbon dioxide emissions by 10 per cent (compared to 1996 levels) by 2016'.

Most authorities do not establish such targets, because it is difficult to set appropriate targets in the absence of much baseline environmental information, because target-setting is a political process which needs to balance environmental and economic criteria, and because any authority has only a limited influence on the achievement of environmental targets. For instance, even the best land-use plan cannot of itself achieve sustainable development or protect nature conservation interests: the broad locational strategies established in the plan are interpreted more specifically in local plans, and these in turn are put into effect by a wide range of players. Actions of the national government (eg road construction or energy privatisation), quasi-national government organisations (eg river catchment plans), developers and a host of other organisations can affect a PPP's impact on the environment. Chapter 9 gives an example of the difficulty involved in unilaterally appraising a PPP which is influenced by external factors. On the other hand, targets can provide an inspiration for action, and an indication of the scale, rather than simply the direction, of change expected. They establish a framework against which the PPP's efficacy can be judged, and ultimately simplify the monitoring and review of the effectiveness of the PPP. Targets must be realistic, however, otherwise they become an embarrassing symbol of defeat rather than a positive goal.

Environmental objectives may be 'strong' or overriding, with decisions being environment-led or strongly constrained by environmental factors; Hertfordshire's structure plan (Chapter 9) is an example where sustainable development is the dominant theme. Objectives may be binding, effectively becoming constraints: such objectives could include the achievement of environmental standards, legal requirements and international agreements. Alternatively, the environmental objectives may be 'incremental' or 'weak' when, for instance, within a framework of non-environmental objectives they aim to ensure that the least environmentally harmful option is chosen (Wilkinson et al, 1994). In these systems, environmental considerations may be traded off against some other objective to generate the optimal result. The SEA process used to appraise a PPP is likely to mirror the PPP objectives: a 'strong' SEA system for 'strong' environmental objectives, an 'incremental' system for 'incremental' objectives.

Finally, no PPP exists in a vacuum. It is influenced by higher-level PPPs and ideologies, and in turn influences other PPPs and projects. Ideally (eg in the 'objectives-led' model), an SEA for the relevant policy would be carried out first, and its objectives and SEA would inform the subsequent preparation of first plans, then programmes and finally projects. This would have the advantages of coordinated decision-making, and of incorporating environmental consider-ations fully at all levels of decision-making. This process of SEA tiering would also be beneficial from a planning perspective: SEA can help to implement and facilitate PPP tiering, and in turn PPP-tiering facilitates SEA and increases its effectiveness.

In sum, a PPP's objectives can be described by listing the objectives where these are known; identifying objectives in discussions with the competent authority and the public; deducing objectives from other sources; separating ultimate from intermediate objectives; and/or linking the PPP's objectives to those of higher- and lower-level PPPs.

Identifying alternative PPPs

Different PPPs may fulfil the stated objective(s) more or less effectively, or may embody different balances of objectives. Developing and comparing alterna-tive PPPs allows the decision-maker to determine which PPP is the best option: which achieves the objective(s) at the lowest cost or greatest benefit to the envi-ronment or sustainability, or which achieves the best balance between contradictory objectives. Alternatives can include:

- the 'do nothing' or 'continue with present trends' option;
- demand reduction, for instance reducing the demand for water through water metering, as well as meeting demand;
- different locational approaches, for instance building new houses in existing towns or in new towns (see Chapter 11);
- provision of different types of development which achieve the same objective, for instance producing energy by gas, coal, wind etc.;
- fiscal measures such as toll roads or congestion charges; and
- different forms of management, for instance waste management by recycling, incineration etc (see Chapter 7).

Alternatives could include indicative combinations of development and man-agement approaches which exemplify themes, such as more public vs more car transport (Scottish Office, 1994). The final alternative chosen could be a still different combination. The range of possible alternatives may be so great that only the most extreme alternatives might be analysed initially to provide the widest indication of possible impacts. The higher-level the PPP, the more strate-gic the alternatives are likely to be: policy-level alternatives may focus on broad approaches to a problem, whilst programme-level alternatives may consider different clusters of projects which achieve the chosen policy.

Some alternatives may need to be considered as a group. For example, the

Dutch electricity supply structure plan involves deciding the location of large power stations, the choice of fuel at each site, the generating capacity for each type of fuel and the possibility of decentralising generation. The development of decentralised power generation affects the choice of siting, fuel and transmission line, so that those alternatives need to be grouped (Verheem, 1992).

Any alternative considered in an SEA should be realistic. The alternatives should represent a range of relatively likely approaches to the objectives identified, and should fulfil all the constraints identified. Generally, alternatives are identified through discussions between experts, perhaps also using techniques such as cost–benefit analysis and goals achievement matrices. However, alternatives may also be identified by the public; for instance the SEA for vegetation management in the Ozark/Ouachita Mountains (US Dept of Agriculture, 1990) considered a low-herbicide alternative based on the results of public consultation.

Describing the PPP

Describing the PPP involves explaining what the PPP really 'means', how it is likely to 'look' once implemented. This is probably the most difficult part of an SEA, in part because many SEAs begin with this stage, rather than with a clear statement of the PPP's objectives.

The higher-tier the PPP is, the more difficult it may be to describe. As a result, the description of policies may be very broad-brush, whilst programme descriptions may be almost as detailed as those in project EIAs. However, there are some ways to describe even a high-tier PPP more precisely. The PPP could be broken down into sectors (eg a regional development plan's approaches to transport, recreation etc); activities (eg a flood alleviation programme's approach to building flood walls, channel reprofiling, flood diversion channels); or phases (eg the development and implementation phases of a new technology; see Chapter 8). The SEA then needs to reappraise the PPP in a holistic manner, taking into account both impacts and mitigation measures appropriate to the overall PPP; otherwise the analysis risks remaining at the sub-component level.

The time-scale over which the PPP is expected to operate should also be stated: whether it has, for instance, a 10-year cycle (like many British land-use plans or the Dutch national waste management programme) or a broad 50-year approach (like the policies of the US Forest Service). The longer the time-scale, the more likely the PPP can incorporate issues of sustainable development and carrying capacity, but the greater the uncertainty associated with predicting its impacts.

Generally, PPPs are described through written explanations and/or maps. These descriptions can include:

- assumptions about the development occurring as a result of the PPP in various years;
- a list of measures for the implementation of a broad 'strategy' or 'vision' (see Chapters 9 and 12);
- maps of routes/corridors for linear development programmes (Chapter 6);
- maps showing zones of future development, for instance new or expanded areas of future urban development in land-use plans; and
- maps showing areas of environmental constraints where development should be restricted (see Chapter 8).

Scoping

The aim of scoping is to identify the key environmental issues that will influence decision-making, and how they will be appraised. Scoping is thus probably the most crucial step in ensuring that the SEA is feasible and useful. The scoping process for a PPP is considerably more complex than that for a project, as a PPP involves multiple activities, is likely to have greater and more diverse impacts over a larger area, be subject to more legislation and policies, and open to a wider range of alternatives. However, although the range of potential environmental impacts that a PPP may have is enormous, only a few of these will be crucial to decision-making. The rest, if considered in the SEA, will cost time and money with minimal additional benefit.

For instance, of all the possible impacts that a trans-European rail network might have, only spatial impacts, primary energy consumption, air and noise pollution, and safety were felt to be crucial for decision-making and thus addressed in the SEA (see Chapter 6). Similarly, the SEA for a chemical waste disposal programme (US Dept of the Army, 1988) argued that significant impacts were only likely to arise in the case of accidental releases of the chemicals, so only an accident scenario was investigated.

Different 'scales' of PPPs (eg national, local) could address different types of impacts. This is implied by the UK Department of the Environment's (1993) good practice guide on environmental appraisal of development plans, which divides impacts into local, natural resource/regional and global, as shown in Table 3.1. Thus, for instance, an international-level SEA could focus primarily on global issues, and a local SEA could emphasise local ones, in a form of subsidiarity. However, larger-scale SEAs still need to address more local issues which, cumulatively, could be significant on a larger scale. For instance, although a national-level SEA may primarily focus on national- and international-level designated sites, it will need to consider cumulative impacts on more local sites. Similarly, a local-level SEA will need to address global issues such as biodiversity, since it is action at these local levels that, cumulatively, leads to global-level change.

Table 3.1 *Division of Environmental Components into 'Scales'*

Global sustainability	Natural resources	Local environmental quality
• transport energy efficiency: trips • transport energy efficiency: modes • built environment energy efficiency • renewable energy potential • rate of CO_2 'fixing' • wildlife habitats	• air quality • water conservation and quality • land and soil quality • minerals conservation	• landscape and open land • urban environmental 'liveability' • cultural heritage • public access to open space • building quality

Source: UK DoE, 1993

It may be possible to identify environmental components that are unlikely to be affected, or likely to be affected particularly strongly, by PPPs for specific sectors, as does Canada's class assessment procedure. This technique can facilitate the scoping process, and should thus be researched further. However, it runs the risk of either being too 'cautious' and thus not eliminating any environmental components from consideration in SEA, or conversely being too prescriptive and not sensitive enough to case-by-case variations.

The scoping stage also needs to address the spatial units over which impacts are addressed. Several types of geographic units are likely to be used: administrative (eg nation, local authority), natural resource-related (eg watershed, airshed), or PPP-related (eg within a given distance from the PPP, where this location is known). Available data are often based on administrative boundaries, whilst the PPP is likely to have effects on natural resource-related areas. Different administrative areas may collect environmental data differently (see Chapter 6), causing further problems.

Scoping techniques include the use of checklists, comparison with the impacts of other similar PPPs, literature surveys, overlay maps, public consultation and expert judgement (CEC, 1994). Any SEA should clearly explain why some impacts have been 'scoped out' and are not addressed in the SEA.

Establishing Environmental Indicators

Indicators are tools for measuring and representing environmental trends. In SEA, indicators can be used to measure and describe baseline environmental conditions and predicted impacts, compare alternatives and monitor the implementation of the PPP vis-à-vis the PPP's objectives. Environmental indicators are generally of three types: state-of-the-environment indicators (eg NO_x levels) which measure the present environmental baseline, impact or pressure indicators (eg NO_x emissions) which measure human impacts on the environment; and action indicators (eg percent of cars with catalytic converters) which measure whether and how various agents have carried out specific actions. The last of these indicators is linked to the implementation of environmental measures as part of a PPP, rather than to the PPP's environmental objectives per se.

Indicators are becoming widely used as tools for sustainable development. For instance, various local authorities in the UK have established environmental or sustainability indicators, and the UK Department of the Environment is establishing indicators as part of its sustainable development strategy. In California, indicators related to structural and functional attributes of ecosystems are used to measure cumulative environmental change.

Indicators can be based on the PPP's environmental objectives, relevant environmental regulations, or existing monitoring programmes. The choice of indicators used in a given SEA should ensure that the indicators:

• are individually and collectively meaningful;
• represent key issues;
• reflect both national/regional interests and local trends;
• are based on valid principles and assumptions;
• are based on relatively easy to collect information, preferably information that has already been available over a reasonable time-scale;
• allow qualitative and quantitative information, and information at different spatial scales, to be used in a methodologically sound way;
• allow consideration of alternatives, both separately and in combination;
• lead to the measurement of baseline information and the prediction and monitoring of impacts;
• yield results that are repeatable given certain explicit assumptions;
• stimulate the imagination of decision-makers and increase insight into the choices to be made; and
• yield results that are understandable to decision-makers and the public (LGMB, 1996; Fergusson and Wilkinson, 1995).

Describing the Baseline Environment

The aim of a baseline description is to identify the current state of the environment, against which the PPP's expected impacts can be appraised: the PPP's impacts are hence measured as the difference in the status of the environment with and without the development. It also identifies environmental problems and provides information for subsequent use in impact prediction and monitoring. Describing the baseline environment thus involves describing the existing environmental baseline and likely future baseline without the PPP in the relevant area, in enough detail to assist in subsequent stages of the SEA process. The baseline description is generally linked to the environmental indicators, and focuses on the key environmental components identified during the scoping process.

The level of detail and quantification needed for the baseline environment description will vary with the tier of the PPP and the availability of appropriate data. Environmental descriptions for a local or programme SEA are likely to be more detailed than those for a national-level or policy SEA. For some programmes, a baseline description similar to that for projects may be feasible. In other cases, where a wide range of activities is being analysed, the baseline description may have to be very broad-brush.

Collecting and analysing baseline data for SEA is often problematic. The large areas and wide range of impacts that are relevant to most SEAs are not covered by most existing sources of baseline information, and do not easily lend themselves to SEA-specific fieldwork. Existing data may be based on only a few sampling points, may be inconsistent between regions or countries, and may not match the boundaries relevant to the PPP. Historical data may be disrupted. There may be problems of confidentiality. On the other hand, the amount of data appropriate for SEA is increasing rapidly, due to, for instance, monitoring systems set up as part of Agenda 21 activities, the increasing refinement and affordability of remote sensing information and rapid advances in GIS (see Chapter 4).

Environmental baselines are constantly changing. The baseline description should thus also include predictions of likely further environmental conditions. Future environmental conditions without the PPP can be predicted based on, for instance, an extrapolation of existing trends, local authority development plans, waste disposal and minerals plans, transport policies and programmes, or employment forecasts. A range of future baseline conditions can be described using different scenarios. Scenarios can include a 'no action' scenario which represents existing trends extrapolated into the future (Chapter 6); other assumptions about future changes in parameters such as population growth, traffic growth or waste generation; or a deliberately planned sequence of events such as the management of different quantities and types of waste (Chapter 7).

The final stage of scoping and baseline description is an identification of likely problem areas, in particular environmental components that are, or will be, at or near their carrying capacity within the lifetime of the PPP. This allows the PPP to be modified so as to prevent or minimise these problems.

Various techniques have been used to describe environmental baselines. The simplest is a written description. Maps can be used to show areas of environmental importance and/or sensitivity. GIS provides an excellent tool for the analysis of data in pre-existing datasets, and its visual nature makes it a highly effective tool for communication; however, the costs of collating, verifying, correcting and manipulating such datasets may limit its applicability.

Predicting Impacts

Impact prediction involves determining the type and magnitude of impacts that the PPP is likely to have on the baseline environment. The range of impacts determined by a PPP will normally be much wider ranging than those of projects, since PPPs generally affect larger areas and result in a greater number and variety of products (plans, programmes, projects or other actions). The impacts of a PPP can be:

- large or small, affecting an international, national, regional or local area;
- positive or negative;
- short-term or long-term, reversible or irreversible;
- direct or indirect;
- cumulative;
- induced/generated by the PPP;
- likely or unlikely to occur;
- distributional (ie affecting different areas or groups of receivers differently; see Chapter 8);
- easy or difficult to mitigate.

A particular aim of SEA may be to assess indirect and cumulative impacts, which the individual, case-by-case approach in project EIAs makes difficult to do adequately (Thérivel et al, 1992; Partidário, 1994). Impact predictions should be clearly linked to the key issues identified during the scoping stage and should relate to the environmental conditions of the affected area. Chapter 9 gives a particularly nice example of this link between environmental problems and impact predictions. The level of detail in which a PPP's impacts are analysed will generally be lower than for a project. In many cases only a very simple indication of the type and level of future impacts will be needed.

A PPP's impacts usually take the form of changes to actions in the following tiering level of actions: 'In practice the impact of [PPPs] on final effects is not calculated: the calculation often stops somewhere "halfway" down the effects network' (CEC, 1994). It may thus be more appropriate to focus on causal factors affecting the environment (for instance energy consumption) rather than on their environmental effects (carbon dioxide emissions).

A range of techniques can be used to predict and represent the impacts of PPPs:

- checklists which show whether the PPP has an impact or not, sometimes with further details on, for instance, impact type (positive, negative) and magnitude;
- compatibility or consistency assessment, which tests whether different sub-components of the PPP are internally consistent (see Chapter 9);

- scenario analysis;
- overlay maps or GIS showing, for instance, sites affected by the PPP (Chapter 4);
- various index, indicator and/or weighting methods such as the Habitat Sustainability Index (Chapter 8);
- computer models, for instance models which predict likely air pollution based on assumptions regarding vehicle type, number, occupancy rate, and fuel use; and
- expert opinion.

Impact prediction in SEA can involve high levels of uncertainty regarding such issues as how the PPP will be translated into projects and actions on the ground, the likely future state of the environment, the effects of other PPPs and projects, carrying capacities and changes in future technology or political and economic priorities. On the other hand, SEA requires discipline and a scientific approach where possible. Many of the techniques for reducing and communicating uncertainty in project EIAs can also be used in SEA. These include:

- clarifying assumptions about, for instance, the environmental impacts of other PPPs;
- stating predictions in terms of ranges rather than giving precise figures, to reflect the uncertainty;
- basing predictions on different scenarios which reflect possible future events and conditions;
- using worst-case scenarios based on the precautionary approach;
- preparing contingency plans;
- carrying out sensitivity analyses, to ensure that changing the assumptions on which predictions are based does not overly influence the outcome of the predictions; and
- triangulation using several of these methods.

Evaluating Impacts and Comparing Alternatives

Evaluating impacts involves taking the 'objective' predictions of the magnitude and type of likely future impacts and making an evaluation (by necessity subjective) about whether these impacts are significant. It also involves testing whether the predicted impacts are in line with the PPP objectives. Significance is generally defined as a combination of the PPP's magnitude/type and the sensitivity or importance of the receiving environment, with the evaluation being based on expert judgement (see Figure 3.1).

The sensitivity of the receiving environment will vary according to the use of the area and the impact in question. In many cases, site designations for

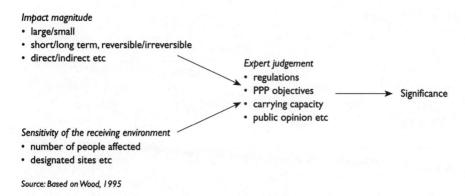

Impact magnitude
- large/small
- short/long term, reversible/irreversible
- direct/indirect etc

Expert judgement
- regulations
- PPP objectives
- carrying capacity
- public opinion etc

Significance

Sensitivity of the receiving environment
- number of people affected
- designated sites etc

Source: Based on Wood, 1995

Figure 3.1 *Impact Evaluation*

wildlife, landscape or archaeological interest may indicate the locality of sensitive environments. 'Tranquil areas' unaffected by major visual or noise intrusion could be another example. The more people live in an area, the greater the sensitivity to human-related impacts such as traffic and noise will be.

The determination of significance can be based on such criteria as regulations and guidelines, the PPP objectives, issues such as sustainability or carrying capacity, equity, and/or public opinion. A simple example of the relationship between the magnitude of the impact, the sensitivity of the receiving environment and the significance of the impact is shown at Table 3.2.

Impact evaluation involves many assumptions and value judgements, which can affect the results of the SEA. The existing concern about bias in project EIAs (DoE, 1991; Glasson et al, 1995) can only be exacerbated with SEA. However, clarifying the assumptions and values inherent in impact evaluations, and making the evaluations in as methodical a fashion as possible, will go a long way towards dealing with these problems. A trial run using the current PPP (if it exists) may help to iron out some of these difficulties and identify possible changes in the future plan. The most common technique for communicating the findings of impact evaluation is a matrix which summarises various aspects of each impact's significance, such as scale, likelihood of occurrence and contentiousness of the issue.

Perhaps the most effective way of evaluating whether a given PPP is optimal in economic, social and environmental terms is to compare it against other PPPs. This clarifies the relative importance of the various objectives, and makes the decision-making process more transparent. The most common way of comparing alternatives is in a matrix, with the alternatives on one axis and environmental components on the other (see Chapter 7). These matrices can be quantitative and precise or descriptive, can include rankings of options or can boil down expert judgement into a few symbols.

The final choice of the alternative to pursue is a political process which bal-

Table 3.2 *Significance Based on Magnitude and Sensitivity: a Simple Possible Approach*

		Magnitude of the impact		
		high	medium	low
Sensitivity of the receiving environment	high	particularly significant	particularly significant	significant
	medium	particularly significant	significant	insignificant
	low	significant	insignificant	insignificant

ances out the economic, social and environmental effects of a PPP. However, techniques for identifying more environmentally friendly alternatives include ranking or pairwise comparison of the impacts of the alternatives, various weighting methods and expert judgement. The results of this exercise may be presented in the SEA report, or may remain internal and confidential.

Mitigation

The SEA process aims to minimise any negative impacts of the preferred PPP to the point where they are no longer significant, to maximise positive impacts and to enhance the environment where possible. Mitigation measures can be defined as measures that avoid, reduce, repair or compensate for a PPP's impacts (DoE, 1989). Broadly, avoidance of impacts is preferable, in turn, to reduction, repair or compensation on both environmental/social and cost grounds.

A major advantage of SEA over project EIA is that it allows consideration of a wider range of mitigation measures, particularly measures to avoid impacts, at an earlier, more appropriate stage of decision-making. Mitigation measures at the PPP level can generally be more strategic, more proactive and more varied than those at the project level. For instance, SEA allows sensitive environmental areas to be avoided during plan-making, rather than to be considered on an ad hoc, reactive basis for each development proposal. It may allow some of the potential negative impacts of one action (eg spoil from tunnel construction) to be used positively for another development (eg landscaping for a new town). It can also allow for a wider range of positive measures to be taken, for instance the creation of new recreation areas or wildlife corridors that go beyond individual development sites.

Possible mitigation measures for PPPs are:

- planning future developments to avoid sensitive sites (Chapter 4);
- placing constraints on, or establishing a framework for, lower-tier PPPs. This could include requirements for SEA/EIA of lower-tier PPPs and projects, or specific requirements for the implementation of projects resulting from the PPP (Chapter 12);
- establishing, or funding the establishment of, new areas of nature conservation or recreation;
- establishing management guidelines for the implementation of the PPP (Chapter 8); and
- relocating sensitive/rare wildlife species or habitats, or local amenities.

Mitigation measures can be identified through consultation with environmental authorities and the public, round tables of experts, and reviews of previous EIAs and SEAs.

Some of these measures may impose additional economic or social costs of their own, or even costs on other aspects of the environment. For instance, using residuals of waste incineration in road construction may reduce the environmental impact of waste management but may lead to environmental problems in the road construction (Verheem, 1994). Once the mitigation measures have been proposed, the impact of the mitigated PPP should be re-evaluated, and this cycle should be continued until no significant negative impacts remain.

Monitoring

Monitoring the PPP has several aims. It tests whether the PPP is achieving its objectives and targets/benchmarks. It identifies any negative impacts requiring remediation. It helps to ensure that mitigation measures proposed in the SEA are implemented. It gives feedback to assist in impact predictions for future SEAs. Monitoring thus needs to refer back to the environmental baseline, impact predictions, and mitigation measures. The environmental indicators identified earlier in this chapter (state of the environment, impacts on the environment and human activities affecting the environment) can be used for monitoring.

In many cases, related monitoring data are already being collected for other purposes: for instance, air pollution emissions may be collected as part of integrated pollution control requirements, or wildlife may be monitored for biodiversity action plans. In other cases, specific monitoring schemes will need to be established.

However, despite the importance of monitoring, its practice is limited. Chapter 11 presents one of the few existing examples.

Conclusions

This chapter does not purport to present a comprehensive 'best-practice' SEA methodology, but rather reviews good practice methodology used to date. Existing SEA techniques have developed from policy appraisal, plan-making and EIA practice, but 'best-practice' SEA methodology will undoubtedly further evolve and diversify in the future. Techniques such as GIS, computer models for predicting the air and noise impacts of traffic, and cheaper and more user-friend-ly photomontage packages are being developed extremely rapidly. Procedural approaches to SEA are developing equally fast. There have been enormous advances in SEA methodology over the last three years, and the next three years will undoubtedly bring even more.

Part II

Sectoral SEAs

4
SEA of Wind Farms in the Soest District (and Other German SEAs)

Volker Kleinschmidt and Dieter Wagner

Introduction

German EIA regulations, like EC Directive 85/337, apply only to development projects. Plans and programmes are not subject to EA, except where they relate directly to a project. However, environmental impacts are taken into account in developing plans and programmes. In 1975 the German government decided that government departments should consider the environmental impacts of plans and programmes associated with public tasks, a first step in the direction of SEA (German Government, 1975). This process is carried out not within the formal EIA system, but independently, and usually without public participation. However it has been applied in practice only relatively rarely.

When, in 1990, the European Commission proposed a draft directive to apply EA to policies, plans and programmes, the German government stated that this application should be limited to plans and programmes which have legally binding effects on subsequent actions and projects, for instance development plans (land-use plans for construction projects). In the case of other plans and programmes, a formal requirement for SEA could lead to a loss of needed flexibility. However, despite this relatively negative official position, a series of research projects and pilot projects were carried out to allow environmental impacts to be better considered at the level of plans. In particular, cities and communities gained considerable experience in preparing 'voluntary' EAs. Now these experiences need to be systematically evaluated to determine their limitations and priorities for subsequent research, and to assist in the evolution from a primarily theoretical to a more practically oriented discussion.

This chapter first reviews the SEA carried out for locating wind farms in the Soest district, then discusses a range of other German research and pilot projects on SEA. The Soest district is a primarily agricultural region of approximately 1500 square kilometres in the state of North Rhine-Westphalia in western Germany.

Background

Construction of wind farms has been an attractive proposition in Germany, since the act on the release of privately produced electricity into public networks (Stromeinspeisungsgesetz), which came into force on 1 January 1991, requires a buyback of 90 per cent of the final price of electricity for renewable energy installations. The extension of the '100 MW Programm Wind' to the '250 MW Programm Wind' also means that developers can apply to the Ministry for Research and Technology for payment of up to DM90,000 for construction of a wind turbine. In addition to these financial incentives, the turbines themselves are becoming increasingly efficient in their use of wind energy. Wind farms can be economically run at average annual wind speeds of only about 4 metres per second or more. Thus, even inland and at low wind speeds such installations can be operated economically.

However, wind turbines, and particularly groupings of turbines into wind farms, have an impact on the landscape through their location on wind-exposed, widely visible areas. They can also cause other negative impacts such as bird strikes and noise. Taking the German government's carbon dioxide reduction programmes and the commitments of the Berlin global climate summit of 1995 seriously, and trying to contribute to the reduction of consumption of raw materials caused by conventional energy production, means seriously considering siting wind farms at ecologically less sensitive locations, using SEA. Land-use zoning concepts for wind farms have already been developed for coastal areas, due to the greater ecological burden they have faced to date. The coastal Länder of Niedersachsen and Schleswig-Holstein, as well as Rheinland-Pfalz, have enacted regulations that identify areas which are not available for the construction of wind farms, using exclusion or optimisation criteria. Different minimum distances between wind farms and the nearest human habitation or ornithological site are given for different land uses. A similar decree is presently being developed in North Rhine-Westphalia. The applicability of these existing zoning concepts and criteria to inland areas is tested here.

More than 70 applications for the installation of wind turbines or wind farms have been forwarded in the last year just to the Soest district council. In the state of North Rhine-Westphalia, in the last two years, proposals for a total of 28,806 kilowatts have been made. Because of this increase in applications, the affected communities are also trying to identify locations for wind farms within their development plans.

Methodological Starting Point

Due to the high number of applications for wind turbines and wind farms in Soest, the Soest district has commissioned a team composed of researchers from the consultancy PRO TERRA TEAM (Dortmund), the University of Dortmund, and the climatology working group of the University of Bochum to develop an SEA framework study for wind power developments. This study should not only contribute to reactive decisions regarding individual applications for wind farms – particularly in view of the Nature Conservation Regulations of 1990 – but should also proactively steer investment in wind farms in the entire district by establishing criteria for an ecologically oriented, land-use-based approach to wind farm siting. The basis of these criteria were those established by Schleswig-Holstein and Niedersachsen along with those of Rheinland-Pfalz and the Soest district framework study.

The study was conducted in two phases. The first (pilot) phase involved determining where wind farms could be located. At this phase, only immediately or relatively rapidly available data were used because, due to the pressure of the task, only three months was allowed for working on the problem. The criteria of Table 4.1 were used to screen the district's sensitivity regarding wind power uses. First, annual average wind speed at ten metres above ground for the Soest district was calculated, based on an evaluation of wind measurements over time (approximately ten years), relative altitudes and surface roughness derived from real land use. Second, the study identified various areas, based on the basic impacts of wind farms:

- excluded areas: areas which would not be available for wind farm developments for reasons of their designations, use or assessed value;
- restricted areas: areas where wind farms are not unreservedly supported and must usually be environmentally assessed through a (short) report;
- favoured areas: areas where no landscape or ecological concerns exist, and where economic conditions (ie sufficient wind speeds) are met.

The assessment of these areas involved identifying conflicts between wind power generation and the land use designations in regional plans, conservation areas and ecologically valuable areas. The study was carried out with help of the GIS system ARC/INFO, which allowed for rapid and flexible manipulation of data. For the meteorological section, the programme WA^{S}P was used.

The second phase of the project should describe the likely environmental impacts of wind farms for existing locations which are desirable in planning terms and suggest possible mitigation measures. In this phase, the Soest district's wind speed should also be calculated at a height of 30 metres, since a survey of all the wind turbine manufacturers in Germany suggested that this corresponds more closely to the average height of the hub (around which the blades pivot) of the newer, larger installations.

Table 4.1 *Comparison of Various Concepts for the Spatial Organisation and Treatment of Wind Farms*

Niedersachsen 1991	Rheinland-Pfalz 1992	Schleswig-Holstein 1991	Framework SEA for wind farms in the Soest District
Suitability criteria			
average annual wind speed of 5 m/s at 10 m height, and possibly areas with 4.5 m/s annual average wind speed, ie ≤4–7 km from 5 m/s isoline		average annual wind speed of 5 m/s at 10 m height; minimal topographical roughness; no area of particular nature value	average annual wind speed of 4.5 m/s at 10 m height
		convenient area for infrastructure works	≥5 km distance between wind farms
		area secured for development	area zoned for commercial or industrial use, or near agricultural concerns
			close to energy grid
Exclusion criteria			
nature conservation areas	nature conservation areas	nature conservation areas	nature conservation areas/ areas for the protection of nature
national parks	central zones of national parks	national parks	
50 m from transmission lines of ≥30 kV	natural monuments	protected areas of landscape	bird migration corridor (2nd stage)
100 m from electricity transmission corridors and broadcasting installations	parts of landscape worthy of protection	other protected areas	
outside safety zone of military installations		coastal sandy moorlands	of very sensitive landscapes
≥200 m from forests		the islands Amrun, Föhr and Sylt	(2nd stage)
200 m from standing water of >5000 m², and from rivers and streams		areas in front of seawalls	75 m from electrical transmission corridors
200 m from seawall		steep shores	
		bird nesting and feeding areas, and bird migration areas	

Restriction criteria		
areas protected by nature conservation law	50 m from transmission lines of ≥30 kV	landscape protection area
	50–100 m from electrical transmission corridors	landscape conservation area
	outside safety zone of military installations	floodplains
	200 m from forested areas	health resort/spa
	50 m from 1st class rivers with buffer zones	relaxation/convalescence area
	300–500 m from protective seawall	recreation area
	50 m from other seawall	nationally and regionally important biotopes
	landscape protection area	Sec 20 biotopes
		areas with rare or endangered bird species
		areas with regionally rare bird species
		areas with great structural diversity, or sensitive landscapes

Source: Based on Kleinschmidt et al, 1994

Characteristics of Wind Power Installations

In contrast to conventional ways of generating electricity, wind farms usually impact only the project site. Impacts such as those that arise during the extraction or transport of fossil fuels or radioactive materials, or through the disposal of wastes accumulated during the conversion of gas into energy, are not at issue. The replacement of conventional power stations with wind farms would reduce emissions of carbon dioxide and toxic substances such as dust and nitrogen oxides, as well as the risk of accidents, eg through the transport of oil, gas or nuclear fuel rods. However, wind farms still have the following negative impacts:

*   electromagnetic disturbance of radio and television transmissions;
*   use of land;
*   noise;
*   impact on birds, particularly bird strikes; and
*   impact on the landscape.

In addition to these potential impacts, further information was collected for the Soest district (see Table 4.2):

*   the mapping of nesting birds in the Soest district (ABU, 1989) indicated the presence of endangered bird species (Red List species), and their frequency in the Soest district;
*   the digitised regional development plan and the map of protected areas in the Soest district indicated areas designated for landscape and nature protection, recreational areas, health resorts, areas for recreation and leisure, flood plains and radio/television transmission corridors;
*   the biotope register of the North Rhine-Westphalia Institute for Ecology, Land Use Development and Forestry indicated biotopes of national, regional and local significance as well as those particularly worthy of protection; and
*   actual land uses were derived from topographical maps of 1:25,000 magnification, and then fed into an ARC/INFO GIS system.

By intersecting the information from several maps, GIS allows all of the information available on these maps to be directly combined. This technique goes beyond the conventional map overlay method, which involves overlaying two maps and transferring the resulting combined information onto a new overlay sheet. Using the combination of the data listed above, the exclusion, restricted and favoured areas could be defined, as shown in Table 4.2. For the definition of the restricted areas, in which most of the criteria were located, four different evaluation groups were constructed, and the results were aggregated into a map.
  Since the assessment of values and significance is not generally arrived at

Table 4.2 *Possible Impacts of Wind Farms*

Criteria for:	land use	noise	landscape impact	bird strike	disturbance of fauna	electromagnetic interference
Exclusion and restricted areas						
electrical transmission corridor						✔
nature conservation areas	✔	✔	✔		✔	
Area for the protection of the natural environment						
scarcity of birds in Soest District	✔			✔	✔	
existence of red list bird species	✔			✔	✔	
structural diversity	✔		✔		✔	
national/regional/local importance	✔		✔	✔	✔	
biotope in accordance with Sec 20 of National Nature Conservation Regs	✔		✔		✔	
area for nature protection	✔	✔	✔		✔	
bird migration route				✔	✔	
Area for the protection of landscape						
landscape conservation area	✔				✔	
landscape protection area	✔		✔		✔	
protected parts of the landscape	✔	✔	✔		✔	
floodplains	✔	✔	✔		✔	
Area for the protection of recreational suitability						
recreation area	✔					
relaxation/convalesence area	✔	✔	✔			
health resort/spa	✔	✔				

Source: Based on Kleinschmidt et al, 1994

solely by scientific analysis, this technique should ideally allow for a personal valuation of the facts. For instance, issues such as how renewable energy production should be weighted against landscape impacts, or what risk of bird strike is acceptable in relation to wind power production, can be addressed. The alternatives were discussed with the advisory committee of the Lower Landscape Authority – in which several NGOs with environmental interests are represented – and with the environment committee. Thus these groups could jointly participate in deciding on the issues.

Results and Conclusions

Approximately 10 per cent (145 km^2) of the district's area was identified as having potential for at least low-wind power installations; that is, they lie in areas with an average windspeed of at least 4 m/sec at a height of 10 m, and areas are identified as excluded, restricted or favoured (see Figure 4.1 and Table 4.3). 2.4% (32.5 km^2) of the district has average wind speeds of more than 4.5 m/sec at a 10 m height. Of the entire land area, 29 per cent was characterised as exclusion areas, 43 per cent as restriction areas and 27 per cent as favoured areas (see Figure 4.2). In particular, 8.8 km^2 were classified as being especially suitable for wind farms, since they are unlikely to be seriously affected by wind farms, and with an average annual wind speed greater than 4.5 km/sec. Intensive use of these areas, with approximately six wind turbines per km^2, could produce more than 11 megawatts of energy.

Inland wind farms are a relatively new phenomenon. Increasingly, investors are willing to construct wind farms as a result of the German government's financial incentives of the '250 MW Programm Wind' and the act legislating the release of privately produced electricity into public networks. Banks are also interested in investing in wind farms in suitable locations, since these enterprises generate profits. Some communities have recognised that wind power can make them more independent and can improve their tight budgets. The proposed zoning model is an example of a sensible, goal-oriented way of combining economic and ecological criteria in the form of an SEA, and can thus contribute to the internationally agreed-on goal of sustainable development.

This technique is also an example of a simple process for allowing participation in the setting of weightings, which both facilitates the ranking of various environment-related goals, and achieves greater acceptance in society. This proactive study also provides an example of an SEA technique which might be useful in other areas of planning, for instance, projects subject to EIA, including wind farms in individual Länder.

The difficult and time-intensive decisions regarding individual projects were, in this case, facilitated through the rapid processing of a spatial zoning concept. The environmental department of the district authority reported in its biannual report of the environment committee that the concept has led to a significant

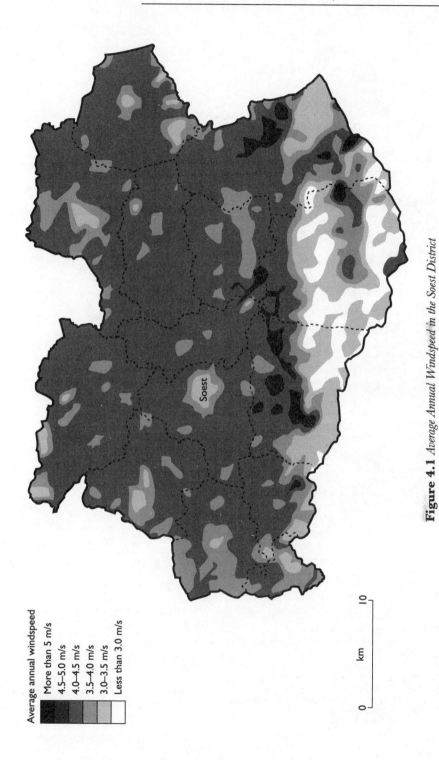

Average annual windspeed

More than 5 m/s
4.5–5.0 m/s
4.0–4.5 m/s
3.5–4.0 m/s
3.0–3.5 m/s
Less than 3.0 m/s

Soest

0   km   10

Figure 4.1 *Average Annual Windspeed in the Soest District*

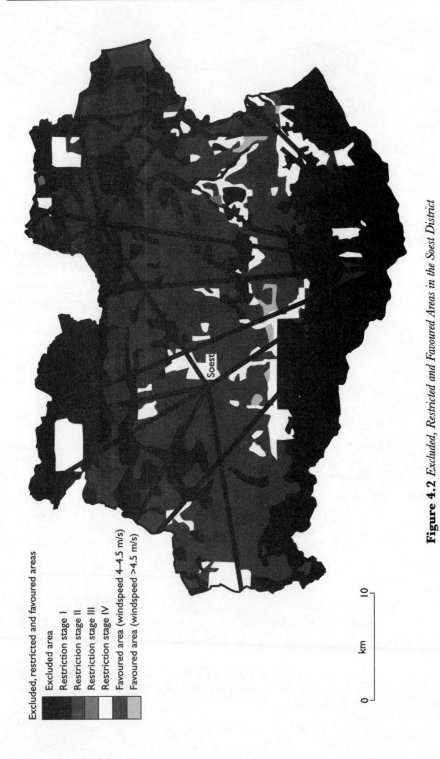

Excluded, restricted and favoured areas

Excluded area
Restriction stage I
Restriction stage II
Restriction stage III
Restriction stage IV
Favoured area (windspeed 4–4.5 m/s)
Favoured area (windspeed >4.5 m/s)

Soest

0   km   10

Figure 4.2 *Excluded, Restricted and Favoured Areas in the Soest District*

Table 4.3 *Area and Lowest Stage of Restriction Corresponding to the Average Annual Windspeed*

Average annual windspeed	Favoured area	Restriction stage IV (affects only few functions worthy of protection)
>5 m/sec	–	0.004 km²
4.5–5 m/sec	8.8 km²	4.5 km²
4–4.5 m/sec	136.6 km²	58.5 km²
3.5–4 m/sec	21.4 km²	15.8 km²

reduction in the time taken to authorise projects.

Certainly there will be further problems to be solved during the second phase of the project. For instance, in the project's first phase, which lasted 2.5 months, not all of the bird migration corridors could be included. The potential landscape impacts in the favoured areas need to be determined more precisely. Coordination with other land-use concepts in the district is also necessary. The study has, however, established an important aid to decision-making, particularly for dealing with wind farms, which promotes the objectives of minimising environmental impacts and intensively promoting the use of renewable energy. The criteria of this study were, at the time of writing, being considered and discussed in a working group of the ministries of urban development and traffic, construction and housing, economic development, and technology, as well as environment, land-use policy and agriculture in North Rhine-Westphalia. A commonly agreed decree is being worked on, to which the author is contributing as an expert on the subject.

A detailed list of German literature on the subject of SEA for wind energy parks has been published by Kleinschmidt et al (1994).

Other SEA Research and Pilot Projects in Germany

Transport Planning

Transport, particularly automotive traffic, can have a considerable effect on the environment. Technical advances have been made in reducing the emissions of individual vehicles, but due to the rising number of vehicles and the increasing size of engines, air pollution has not decreased proportionally. In Germany, EIAs have been carried out for individual road projects since before EC Directive 85/337, and virtually no further methodological improvements can be expected from this direction. The decisive factor is strategic-level planning of the entire transport system. A first example of this is the Federal Transport

Infrastructure Plan 1991–2001, which is a programme of the federal government for the long-term expansion of projects concerning the transport infrastructure – the rail network, national long-distance roads, federal waterways and airports – comprising an investment of about ECU 250 million. Although the programme only encompasses a small proportion of the road network, it accounts for 52 per cent of the total heavy goods vehicle distance travelled; obviously this supra-regional road network strongly influences the subsequent road network. The planning process for the Federal Transport Infrastructure Plan was particularly influenced by the reunification of Germany. New road and rail connections between east and west were expected to be built, and existing ones improved and extended.

The basis for the traffic planning process is a coordinated set of traffic forecasts. These forecasts result in the long-term demand for individual projects. The project proposals are then appraised using cost–benefit analyses, which also take environmental effects into account. Subsequently, an ecological risk analysis is carried out. This evaluation results in a ranking of priorities for individual measures, which are then passed into law. In the case of the Federal Traffic Infrastructure Plan, for the first time the traffic forecasts included some restrictions on traffic growth, for instance higher user costs for the various traffic modes.

Although the methodology for the Federal Transport Infrastructure Plan goes beyond the consideration of individual projects, it still falls short of systems analysis (Wagner and Kleinschmidt, 1995). The application of systems analysis is being considered for the next version of the plan, and use of SEA could then also be possible. It is often argued that the environmental effects of such a multimodal system cannot really be portrayed. Yet these effects can be represented clearly and transparently to decision-makers: for instance, the severance of conservation areas by planned transport corridors can be represented using GIS.

Research Programmes

The German ministry for research and technology promotes technological development and research with approximately ECU7 million per year. These new technologies can have both positive and negative impacts on the environment. It is thus important that, before a decision is made concerning such a 'promotional' programme, the environmental impact of carrying it out should be carefully examined. Even environmentally friendly technologies can have serious environmental effects. For instance, photovoltaic cells are very energy efficient, but the use of cadmium in their production causes considerable waste disposal problems. In the case of photovoltaic cells and power plants, a methodology for assessing their environmental effects was developed (Hirtz et al, 1991) and tested (Huber and Hirtz, 1992).

Land-Use Planning

In Germany, many communities have recently tried to promote environmental protection by carrying out an SEA of their land-use plans. The ministry of the environment is developing a good practice guide for communities based on experience to date. The guide's methodology and the appraisal results are being tested in a practical case study using the city of Erlangen. This case study is also a demonstration project of the European Commission as part of the preparation of the SEA directive (Hübler et al, 1995).

In various communities, programme SEA has also been used to choose new residential or industrial areas (Braun et al, 1994). These appraisals predominantly use overlay techniques to identify and represent environmental conflicts. The following conclusions were drawn from such SEAs for community plans in an entire region and from land-use plans:

- SEAs for lower-tier development plans can concentrate on specific areas, so that less work is needed. SEA can thus reduce the scope of issues which need to be addressed at subsequent stages of planning.
- SEA is generally not politically accepted for plans which are subject to strong political pressure. Even if the implementation of the plan is expected to cause environmental conflicts, SEA is unlikely to contribute to a compromise.
- Development plans with long time horizons are less likely to be subject to much political and public interest, but it is equally unlikely that local authorities will be willing to provide additional resources for SEA.
- SEA is most likely to succeed with a land-use plan with an intermediate time horizon that is not under great political pressure. In these situations SEA can be an active instrument in optimising plan-making, which informs political decisions and helps to build consensus.

Regional/Spatial Planning

Spatial planning plays an important role in Germany: it influences subsequent plans, for instance land-use plans (Jacoby et al, 1994). At the regional planning level, strategic decisions are still possible, so this is a good starting point for SEA. A recent study (Jansen and Wagner, 1993) identified what environmental issues are being addressed by current regional plans and what issues are being omitted. The study concluded that the omissions were due less to missing instruments or a weak legal basis than to deficiencies in their implementation: existing possibilities were not being sufficiently used. The application of SEA is particularly important in this type of situation to ensure that all environmental consequences are taken into account and to control the regional plan's implementation through subsequent plans. Ecological assessments of plans often neglect the time problems involved in developing and agreeing on these plans: by the time this lengthy process has taken place and the plan is operational, many new problems will have emerged, and possibly new knowledge will have been acquired. Thus it is important that the SEA accompanies the entire planning process, through the multiple stages of plan-making.

Assistance to Developing Countries

Since approximately 1987 (after some preliminary work), the German ministry of economic cooperation has had a general obligation to carry out EA for all projects, plans and programmes as part of its practice of technical and financial cooperation with developing countries (Bundesministerium für wirtschaftliche Zusammenarbeit, 1995). This ensures that projects resulting from this cooperation become more environmentally friendly. These projects are often already very complex and are only rarely comparable with projects which require EIA under the EC Directive (such as power stations). They often represent plans and programmes; an example might be a programme to reduce the use of pesticides in Thailand (Kleinschmidt, 1995). However, a systematic environmental evaluation of this entire programme would allow environmental issues to be incorporated not only into individual projects but also into the entire programme of development, as well as the modules for the individual countries.

Conclusions and Prospects

This short overview shows that experiences of, and research concerning, SEA in Germany are available. At the moment there is the danger that, as was the case with project EIA, a lengthy theoretical discourse will be conducted about this instrument and expectations will correspondingly be very high. This is likely to cause resistance amongst practitioners and administrators. The development of appropriate EU guidelines could provide useful pressure towards more systematic and proactively oriented discussions. However, one series of issues should be addressed as soon as possible. These include:

- further development of EA methodologies for SEA;
- coordination of the timing of SEA with the actual timing of plan-making in practice, since the development of plans takes place primarily in cycles;
- the range of information and type of public participation that apply to various types of plans; and
- links between the SEA and subsequent stages of planning.

For SEA to be successful it is important that the mistakes of the implementation of project EIA are not repeated. Further corresponding research work needs to be commissioned, and manuals and trial runs must be developed as training aids. The European SEA workshop planned for September 1996 in Potsdam (Germany) will achieve some preparatory work towards this. However, in an age of tight budgets and deregulation, SEA has little chance if the central task of such proceedings is not made completely clear: improvements in environmental protection at the same time as improvements in the planning process.

Acknowledgements

Particular thanks are due to the Soest district, which commissioned the work on wind farms; the regional authority of Arnsberg and the federal ecological agency (LOEBF) North Rhine-Westphalia for the provision of data; the landscape advisory committee, environment committee and landscape authority of the Soest district for their comments; the climatology working group of the University of Bochum, particularly Dr Steinrücke, for the climatological section; and Dipl-Ing Schauerte-Lüke for his authoritative GIS analysis.

5

SEA of an Environmental Restoration and Waste Management Programme, United States

J Warren Webb and Lorene L Sigal

Introduction

The US Department of Energy (DOE) is preparing a programmatic environmental impact statement (PEIS) to evaluate strategies for integrating environmental clean-up and waste management activities and to plan for a 30-year clean-up programme that protects health and the environment and considers future uses of land. A draft PEIS (DOE, 1995) was issued for public review in September 1995. The comment period ended in December 1995. Currently the majority of environmental restoration and waste management activities are conducted on a site-by-site basis at about 100 DOE facilities across the US (Figure 5.1).

In contrast to a project-level analysis, which generally provides detailed quantitative information on the impacts of a site-specific action and its alternatives, the draft PEIS is an SEA that provides information on broad policy and programmatic alternatives. Although there is quantitative analysis of human health and worker risks for the environmental restoration alternatives, most of the remaining analyses are qualitative, because individual future clean-up decisions cannot be predicted. Analyses for the waste management alternatives are more quantitative, because discerning factors, such as transport of wastes, commitment of land and the suitability of DOE sites for treatment, storage, and disposal facilities, are more readily known.

Concurrently with the Environmental Restoration and Waste Management

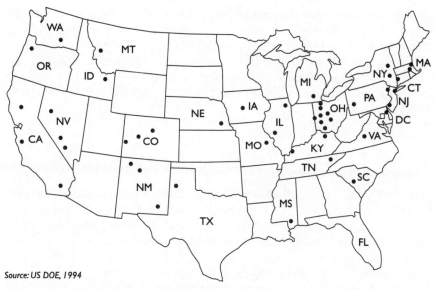

Source: US DOE, 1994

Figure 5.1 *US DOE Environmental Restoration and Waste Management Activity Locations*

Programmatic Environmental Impact Statement (ER&WM PEIS) the DOE is preparing PEISs for reconfiguring its nuclear weapons complex and for managing its spent nuclear fuel. Preparation of these documents is being coordinated with the ER&WM PEIS, which addresses the impacts of the other programmes as part of its cumulative impacts analysis.

Institutional Framework

In the US, SEA is associated with making and implementing policies, plans and programmes by agencies of the federal government and, rarely, by agencies of state government. The National Environmental Policy Act of 1969 (NEPA) requires that

> *all agencies of the Federal Government ... include in ... major Federal actions significantly affecting the quality of the human environment, a detailed statement ... on the environmental impact ... (42 USC Chapter 55, §4332).*

The term 'major Federal action' has been subsequently defined by the President's Council on Environmental Quality, established by NEPA, to include 'programmes [and] rules, regulations, plans, policies, or procedures; and legislative proposals.' As a result, policies, programmes and similar actions by federal agencies are subject to EIA. The resulting documents, EISs and EAs, are referred to as programmatic, regional, cumulative or generic documents. In general, these documents are prepared for groups of actions related geographically or having similarities of project type, timing, media or technological character. So far, NEPA's provisions have not been applied to broad government policies, such as national transportation or energy policy, but this is thought likely to occur in the future. The provisions of NEPA were applied, for example, in President Clinton's timber plan for the Pacific Northwest (USDA/USDOI, 1994).

The NEPA Process

The NEPA process for SEA does not differ from the NEPA process for project-level environmental assessment. However, the timing and scope, the level of detail and degree of quantification may differ. In all cases, NEPA documents are to be prepared early in agency planning when the agency can:

- evaluate a range of alternatives;
- highlight potential environmental problems;
- provide environmental information to public officials and citizens; and
- be used to help make agency decisions before specific commitments are made or actions are taken.

The PEIS process is particularly appropriate for agencies that set national goals and then take discrete steps to accomplish those goals. Subsequently, specific EISs or EAs are prepared for local actions and tiered to the PEIS for description and discussion of the broad programmatic issues and alternatives. The milestones (Table 5.1) for the ER&WM PEIS are typical of the NEPA process for all federal agencies with the exception of the implementation plan, which is a requirement specific to the DOE NEPA process. Other items are required by the Council on Environmental Quality regulations that implement NEPA.

Methodology

Alternatives

In addition to a no-action baseline analysis, the PEIS includes four programmatic alternatives for environmental restoration. The first alternative emphasises compliance with environmental standards determined to be applicable or relevant and appropriate, with utilisation of various treatment and resource recovery technologies to the maximum extent possible. The second alternative involves foreseeable land use to better define likely exposure scenarios and appropriate waste management strategies. The third considers the balance

Table 5.1 *Major Milestones for the US DOE Environmental Restoration and Waste Management PEIS*

Milestone	Date
Notice of Intent to prepare a PEIS published in the *Federal Register* and elsewhere	October 1990
23 public scoping meetings	December 1990 to February 1991
Draft Implementation Plan (IP) issued	February 1992
6 public IP workshops	January to March 1992
IP issued	January 1994
Notice of Availability published in the *Federal Register* and elsewhere; draft PEIS issued	Third Quarter 1994
Public and agency review of the draft PEIS/ public hearings	Fourth Quarter 1994
Final PEIS to be issued	First Quarter 1995
Record of Decision to be published	1995

Source: US DOE, 1994

between remedial worker and transportation risks, and risks to a site's surrounding population. The fourth emphasises foreseeable land use to establish the initial remediation objectives in conjunction with consideration of workers and transportation risks.

The first waste management alternative considered in the PEIS addresses a continuation of the current programme. Other alternatives represent various waste management programme configurations including decentralised, regionalised, and centralised approaches for each of six waste types (ie high-level waste, transuranic waste, low-level waste, low-level mixed waste, hazardous waste, and greater-than-class-C low-level waste).

The following risks and impacts are evaluated for each of the ER&WM alternatives:

- Transportation risk: collision risk; radioactive and hazardous material risk to industrial workers and the public from routine shipments; potential radioactive and hazardous materials risk to workers and the public from spillage during transport.
- Treatment facility risk: risk of construction, operation and potential effluent releases.
- Resource impact: impacts on land, water, energy and construction materials use.
- Recycling impact: potential use of materials for recycling.
- Environmental impact: impacts on air quality, noise, biological resources,

socioeconomic, archaeological resources, surface water and groundwater.
- Near-term risk: industrial, radiological and hazardous material risk to workers and the public during ER&WM programme activities.
- Residual risk: risk to the public from exposure to radioactive and hazardous material remaining at any remediation or decontamination and decommissioning site. If material is moved to another site, residual risk at the new site will be identified.

Assessment

In general, the approach to the assessment of impacts in the ER&WM PEIS is to create models of the contamination problems and the waste management activities across the DOE complex and then consider how the different alternatives affect the models. The comparative information is to be used to guide decision-making for the ER&WM programme.

Environmental Restoration Approach
The approach to assessment of ER alternatives has eight major tasks. The following four preliminary tasks must be completed before the major analyses can begin:

- identification of contamination situations that represent the entire spectrum of actual contamination at more than 7000 sites in the DOE complex;
- identification of available remediation technologies;
- description of remediation technology impacts (eg resource utilisation, releases, effluents, secondary wastes); and
- identification and/or development of risk assessment methodologies (eg for current and future residents near sites, remedial workers, waste transportation personnel, flora and fauna).

Once these tasks are completed, the major analyses include the following:

- The engineering analysis, in which one or a combination of technologies is selected that best address(es) the contamination situation(s) for the alternative under consideration; this results in a conceptual design (remedial situation) for which impacts are evaluated.
- The environmental analysis, in which overall risk, short-term (construction phase) and long-term (residual contamination) ecological impacts, impacts to workers and the public and use of natural resources are evaluated for the conceptual designs.
- A composite (ie cumulative) effects analysis, in which impacts (eg to ecology, land usability and socioeconomics) across the entire DOE complex are assessed once all contamination situations for a specific ER

alternative have been completed.
- A comparison of alternatives, in which the results of the environmental and composite effects analyses are summarised and compared for the following categories:
  - overall risk to human health;
  - relative cost;
  - probability of success;
  - land usability impacts;
  - socioeconomic impacts;
  - short-term impacts on ecology, physical resources and the man-made environment;
  - long-term impacts on ecology, physical resources and the man-made environment; and
  - cumulative impacts.

Because of the magnitude of the assessment, unit risk factors are developed for contaminants in each environmental setting in the DOE complex and for worker and transportation risk. The risk factors for public risk caused by residual contamination are used to calculate approximate installation-wide total risk to the public from ER activities. For the alternatives emphasising land use, bounding land use options (ie unrestricted, somewhat restricted and totally restricted) have been developed, and each contamination situation is evaluated as though it would be remediated to achieve these bounding conditions. An automated system has been developed that allows the individual contamination situations to be assessed and the impacts combined across an entire facility. The method estimates the volume of soil and water that must be remediated, the size of containment structures that must be built, the amount of transportation required, and the risk, cost and related impacts (eg land disturbance) associated with each programmatic alternative.

Waste Management Approach
The assessment of the WM alternatives focuses on the anticipated amounts of waste for affected DOE facilities and the waste transport requirements of each alternative configuration as the sources of potential environmental impacts. The assessment consists of the following four major tasks:

- identification of existing and future waste types, quantities and locations including ongoing and likely future efforts to reduce waste;
- development of specific waste management facility and transportation requirements for each configuration alternative under a waste type;
- evaluation of the environmental impacts of the waste management facilities and waste transport with a focus on attainment of applicable standards and criteria and on broad environmental resource categories (eg for air, water and land-use impacts); and

- compilation and comparison of impacts for each waste type altern-ative and for combinations of waste type alternatives at a DOE site.

In addition, the environmental impacts of emerging technologies are evaluated and compared with available technologies to determine the desirability of wait-ing for a new technology that may soon be available.

Evidence of Current and Future Effectiveness of SEA

Because the ER&WM PEIS is not yet complete, the effectiveness of DOE's SEA process with regard to all evaluation criteria cannot be analysed. However, effec-tiveness to date can be judged by DOE's efforts to engage the various publics in the planning for the ER&WM programme; DOE's responses to the issues raised by the public during scoping; and DOE's commitment to carry out remediation activities, maintain and improve waste management operations and meet cur-rent health, safety, and environmental requirements.

On 22 October, 1990 a Notice of Intent (NOI) was published in the *Federal Register* announcing DOE's intent to prepare the ER&WM PEIS. The NOI invited interested agencies, affected Indian tribes and the public to participate and, in particular, to submit comments on the scope of the PEIS. The NOI also described DOE's proposed action, alternatives and issues. During the scoping period of 120 days, 23 public meetings were held and more than 1200 people provided approximately 7000 comments on the NOI, either in person at meet-ings or in written form. Although most of the comments came from individuals, some 280 organisations, including environmental, public interest and communi-ty groups, also participated.

Subsequently, a draft ER&WM PEIS Implementation Plan (IP) was pre-pared. The draft IP summarised the comments received and identified those issues, as suggested by the comments, that would be considered in preparing the PEIS. Although not required by the public participation requirements under CEQ and DOE NEPA regulations, the draft IP was made available for public comment on 4 February, 1992 (Table 5.1). The document was mailed to about 2000 individuals who had participated in the scoping process. Six regional IP workshops were held. About 1200 individuals submitted written comments, and about 300 individuals attended the workshops and submitted an additional 1000 written and oral comments. Following the 60-day review period, the comments were summarised, additional issues to be included in the PEIS were identified and a final ER&WM PEIS IP was prepared (DOE, 1994).

In addition, in January 1992, DOE chartered an Environmental Restoration and Waste Management Advisory Committee composed of members selected from universities; trade associations; federal, state and local governments; Native

American organisations and groups; unions; environmental groups; and other interested parties. The committee reviewed the draft IP and submitted an additional 150 comments. The committee will continue to function as an advisory group to the DOE assistant secretary for Environmental Restoration and Waste Management on both the substance of, and the process for, the PEIS from the perspective of affected groups and state and local governments.

The DOE established a tracking system to identify and categorise all comments received during the public participation processes. More than 15,000 comments were categorised into 29 topical issues. Based on number of comments, the most important issues were DOE credibility, public participation and oversight; environmental quality and environmental impacts; occupational and public health; waste management; and management of clean-up activities. The final IP discusses, by topical issue, the comments received on the scope of the ER&WM PEIS and also summarises DOE's responses.

During the public workshops on the draft IP, the DOE made a commitment to discuss issues raised during scoping in the PEIS. Such discussion would help the public understand the decisions reached as a result of the PEIS process and gives the public and interested groups and agencies an opportunity to directly provide input on future improvements to conducting the ER&WM programme.

Future evidence of the effectiveness of the SEA process will be found in public acceptance of the DOE decisions for the ER&WM programme, incorporation of the decisions resulting from the PEIS process into ER&WM planning documents and lack of litigation. Agreement of the US Environmental Protection Agency and state regulators with the DOE environmental clean-up and waste management activities outlined in the PEIS also can be seen as evidence of success. Finally, of course, the ultimate evidence of the effectiveness of the EA process is protection of the environment.

The Influence of SEA on Decision-Making

It is too early in the SEA process to comment specifically on how the ER&WM PEIS influences decision-making. In general, the influence of SEA on decision-making is probably not directly measurable. Certainly it may contribute to better basic planning for policies or programmes by evaluating and summarising environmental and other information for the decision-maker. On the other hand, there are difficulties apparent in the process as applied thus far. For example, it appears that DOE did not evaluate an alternative that is being actively pursued at individual sites – that of privatisation of waste treatment. Even before the PEIS is finalised, some sites are sending waste to commercial concerns or are undertaking their own site-level programmatic analyses to include a commercial treatment option. The integration of SEA with systemwide policy decision-making is clearly still in its infancy. However, it is our opinion that the real value is found in the incremental technical and political decisions that occur throughout the process – before a final decision(s) is reached. For example, issues raised by the public or government agencies are considered and factored into decision-making during the process; alternatives are carefully considered and chosen, and those that have potential for significant environmental impacts are dismissed early in the planning process; and situations that might result in adverse environmental impacts are avoided or reduced to acceptability through mitigation measures. Once established by an agency, the SEA process results in greater environmental awareness on the part of the decision-makers.

SEA Constraints and Opportunities

Constraints

Our experience (Sigal and Webb, 1989) has been that, in general, constraints to the SEA process can be categorised as institutional and methodological. First and foremost, at the institutional level, there must be a commitment to SEA and recognition throughout an organisation of its value. Without such commitment, SEA is nothing but a paper exercise. In recent years, DOE has developed this institutional commitment. The agency currently has four major PEISs in preparation.

In addition, successful SEA requires early planning and inter- and intra-agency cooperation. These are activities that most agencies find difficult to conduct. From the beginning, DOE programme offices responsible for wastes requiring management have worked together to prepare the IP and the draft PEIS. Also, as part of the scoping process, DOE invited other federal agencies to participate as cooperating agencies. The US Department of Human and Health Services, the Nuclear Regulatory Commission and the US Environmental Protection Agency are developing information, preparing environmental analyses and lending staff support. Furthermore, during preparation of the PEIS, DOE will request consultations and coordinate with other federal and state agencies having regulatory authority or technical expertise. (Nonetheless, the difficulties of integrating systemwide policies with those of individual sites, discussed above, have not been entirely avoided.)

Finally, agencies frequently resist SEA because of perceptions of cost and restrictions on action during the process, and poor understanding of timing and scope. Although we do not know the cost of the ER&WM PEIS, a number of studies have been made of the costs of EA as a percentage of total project costs. The results range from about 0.1 per cent upward, seldom exceeding 1 per cent. Such an amount could easily be saved from improved project designs that result from SEA (Webb and Sigal, 1992).

Methodological constraints are usually associated with level of detail and uncertainty. In general, an SEA document is prepared in less detail and with less quantification than documents for specific projects. Where missing, fragmented or unstandardised data preclude quantitative analysis, qualitative comparisons are acceptable. For example, DOE does not expect the ER&WM PEIS analysis to support siting certain waste management facilities at specific DOE sites. Rather, the analysis will identify potential DOE sites within a region in which one or more waste facilities could be located. Subsequent NEPA documents will address the specifics of siting waste management facilities and issues such as capacity, technology (eg process alternatives) and location-specific environmental impacts.

Although SEA does not lend itself to quantitative analyses without making assumptions, particularly in models, that may reduce the accuracy and increase the uncertainty of predictions, these are not insurmountable problems. Decision-makers generally have lower expectations regarding assumptions, uncertainty and precision at the broader levels of government planning. A comparative analysis of alternatives can still highlight potential environmental problems for the decision-maker. In the ER&WM PEIS, DOE recognises that uncertainties inherent in the mixed radiological and hazardous waste contamination problems within its installations make the human health and ecological risk assessment methods a particularly critical element for the environmental restoration recommendations. To ensure quality in these analyses, DOE has selected highly qualified professionals to develop and apply the risk methodologies. Models will be compared with each other, model output will be compared with actual data, and the methods and application will be subject to peer review. In addition, the risk assessment process will incorporate guidelines established by the US Environmental Protection Agency.

Finally, effective and efficient SEA requires an experienced multidisciplinary team of experts. For the ER&WM PEIS, experienced specialists are being used for both preparation and internal review of the document. In addition, independent experts serve on the Environmental Restoration and Waste Management Advisory Committee.

Opportunities

Although agencies have resisted SEA, we believe that decision-makers and the public are realising that a well-prepared, timely PEIS can highlight and anticipate potential environmental problems, prevent future delays in implementation of policies and programmes, assist in long-range planning, and prevent or provide support for agency positions during litigation (Webb and Sigal, 1992). Moreover, SEA is a mechanism for public involvement in the decision-making process that contributes to public acceptance of agency decisions. It also provides opportunities for federal, state, and local agencies to work together so that regulators and decision-makers have a basis for understanding and resolving issues related to agency activities and plans. SEA can integrate activities and planning across agency programmes. For example, the ER&WM PEIS will evaluate the proposed action of implementing an integrated ER&WM programme. Such a programme would enhance the coordination of waste operations, environmental restoration, technology development, and facility transition with other agency programmes generating wastes requiring management, such as defence programmes, nuclear energy and energy research (DOE, 1994).

In the US EIA process, NEPA documents for specific projects within a programme can be tiered to a PEIS. Such tiering allows an agency to avoid duplication of paperwork through the incorporation by reference of general, and relevant, specific discussions from a PEIS into a document of lesser scope. Finally, programmatic documents are the perfect vehicle for assessment of the cumulative impacts of multiple actions that are similar in nature, broad in scope or connected (ie actions that trigger other actions or actions that cannot proceed unless other actions are taken previously or simultaneously) (Sigal and Webb, 1989).

6
SEA of the Trans-European Transport Networks

Ann Dom

The Development of the Trans-European Transport Networks: Integrating Environmental Concerns

According to Title XII of the Treaty on European Union, the trans-European transport networks (TENs) should help to achieve the objectives of completing the single market and ensuring economic and social cohesion, particularly with regard to outlying regions. The establishment of integrated high-quality transport networks throughout the EU and beyond its frontiers is therefore considered a priority task (CEC, 1993a).

The European Commission plays a crucial role in the strategic definition of the TEN. In preparing the multimodal network the Commission has, in close co-operation with the member states, developed various master plans for the revision and extension of the different interregional networks. Between 1990 and 1994, separate documents were published on each of the plans, ie the road network, the rail network (conventional and high-speed rail), the combined transport network, inland waterways and seaports, and the network of airports.

In 1994, the Commission submitted a proposal for a Decision to the European Parliament and the Council on Community guidelines for a multimodal TEN (CEC, 1994). These guidelines constituted a first attempt to initiate a process of integrating all the guidelines specific to each mode of transport in a consolidated diagram, to reflect the EU's vision of what the multimodal trans-European transport network should be by the year 2010. They cover the network schemes for the various modes, the objectives and broad lines of measures for the development process, and identify projects of common interest.

Since the first publication, the guidelines have twice been amended under the co-decision procedure by the European Parliament and the Council of Ministers, and are – at the time of writing – not yet finally approved.

To improve the future environmental performance of the transport sector, the Commission intends to apply SEA as an integral part of the decision-making process for transport infrastructure policies, the TEN in particular. This intention has been stated in several Commission policy papers, although mostly in very general terms. The clearest reference to the SEA of the TEN was made in the White Paper on the Common Transport Policy:

> *Strategic environmental impact assessment will be an integral part of the decision making process for transport infrastructure PPPs and investment decisions on individual projects. In order to provide a level playing field for investment decisions in transport infrastructure, the Community should recommend a standard methodology for their cost-benefit analysis, including externalities, even when the infrastructure in question does not form part of a Trans-European network (CEC, 1992a).*

The theme can again be found in the proposed guidelines (CEC, 1994) which underline that the Commission will undertake SEA – together with socioeconomic assessment – as part of the future network development. According to the text agreed by the Parliament, an SEA will have to be carried out by July 1998, and all future revisions of the TEN master plans must take the results of this SEA into consideration. However, this clause was rejected by the council in June 1995. One of the most recent parliamentary amendments to the proposal reinforces the idea that the establishment and development of the TEN must take account of the need to protect the environment (CEC, 1995).

SEA of the European High Speed Rail Network

The High Speed Rail (HSR) network was the first of the master plans to be published by the Commission in December 1990 (CEC, 1990). The plan has been drawn up with a view to the year 2010, and comprises the (at the time) 12 members states together with Austria and Switzerland. In all, the network consists of ±9,800 kilometres of new lines able to cope with speeds of up to 300 kilometres per hour, and ±14,400 kilometres of upgraded existing lines to handle speeds of 200 kilometres per hour and more. At the time of its publication, the HSR master plan still involved a high degree of abstraction: the exact location of certain new links was not yet known and decisions regarding the choice between new lines or upgraded ones had not all been taken.

The Council Resolution of 17 December 1990 requested the Commission, together with the representatives of the governments of the member states, the railway companies and the railway industry, to look in greater detail at:

- the socioeconomic impact of the network on the integrated transport market and the development of the Community;
- the impact of the network on the environment in the broadest sense, and how it compares with other modes of transport in this regard;
- economic studies, including, amongst other things, the commercial aspects of the key links and other crucial points in the network and the problem of financing them.

Following the resolution, several studies on the network were commissioned by the Commission's Directorate-General for Transport (DGVII). These studies were conducted by different consultants, and resulted in separate reports on each of the above issues, with little or no interaction between the themes.

The SEA of the network was conducted in 1992 by the Belgian consultancy Mens en Ruimte (Mens en Ruimte, 1993). The study was closely followed by a steering group consisting of representatives of DGVII and of the Directorate-General for the environment (DGXI). At several stages, presentations of the study's progress were made to the High Level Group on the development of a European high-speed train network. This group was created by the Commission to assist in creating the outline plan and identifying priority projects, and consists of representatives of the national administrations of the member states, the Community of European Railways, the major manufacturers of railway equipment, Eurotunnel and the Roundtable of Industrialists.

Alternatives and Scenarios Considered

The objective of the SEA was to make a comparative assessment of the environmental effects of the HSR network and of the other modes that are used for the long-distance transport of passengers. Thus, the alternatives considered are the existing networks that are in direct competition with the HSR network, ie:

- the conventional rail network (±25,000 km), which includes the existing interregional conventional rail links and the French *train à grande vitesse* (TGV) line between Paris and Lyons (the only HSR line that was operational in 1988);
- the network of main roads (mostly motorways) parallel to the HSR lines (total length ±31,450 km);
- a selection of 83 airports that provide regular intra-European commercial flights.

The analysis relates to the year 2010, with 1988 as the basic year (the choice of 1988 was based on the availability of traffic data). The evaluation of the impact of the HSR network is performed by comparing scenarios 'with' and 'without' the HSR network.

- The 2010 Reference scenario (2010 REF) corresponds to the situation in which no new HSR lines are constructed, and in which only the 1988 operational HSR lines are included (ie Paris–Lyons).
- The 2010 High-Speed Train scenario (2010 HST) involves the complete realisation of the HSR network as it is proposed by the Commission.
- The 2010 Forced Mobility scenario (2010 FM) has the same high mobility level as the 2010 HST scenario, but uses only conventional traffic modes.

The last scenario was added because the HSR network – in addition to causing important shifts of traffic flows between modes – also generates new traffic (see Figure 6.1). This 'induced' traffic is an immediate result of the fact that the high-speed train makes long-distance journeys more attractive. Thus, the 2010 HST scenario has a mobility level that is about 2.5 per cent higher than the 2010 REF scenario. It was therefore thought important to also make a comparison with a high mobility scenario without an HSR network. The 2010 FM scenario corresponds to the situation in which EC policies should be aimed at increasing mobility by means of conventional modes.

SEA Methodology

The scope of the SEA mainly covers environmental issues that were identified as being of Community interest in the Green Paper on Transport (CEC, 1992b) and the Fifth Environmental Action Programme. The impacts and indicators that were considered in particular are:

- spatial impact: land take (in hectares), barrier effects, impacts on landscape and sensitive sites, effects on the spatial organisation of activities and on the urban environment;
- primary energy consumption;
- carbon dioxide emissions;
- air pollution: emissions of carbon monoxide, nitrogen oxides, sulphur dioxide, volatile organic compounds, particulate matter and their combined acidifying and toxic effects;
- noise pollution in terms of nuisance zones around infrastructure; and
- traffic safety, measured in number of fatalities.

The method was developed to be straightforward and flexible. For most aspects a qualitative analysis has been made together with a quantitative evaluation. However, a quantitative evaluation of the more local aspects (noise pollution

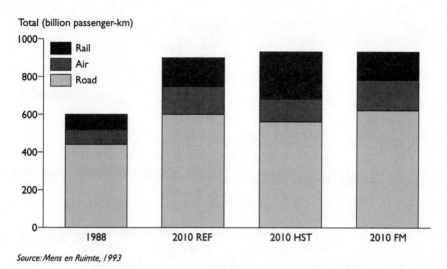

Total (billion passenger-km)

Source: Mens en Ruimte, 1993

Figure 6.1 *Long-distance Passenger Transport: Traffic Volume*

and impact on landscapes and habitats) proved to be difficult at this stage because of the high degree of abstraction of the network and the lack of sufficiently detailed European databases. In the future, SEAs on a corridor level, the logical next step in the SEA process, should allow a better assessment of noise pollution and impact on landscapes and habitats.

The impact assessments take into account vehicle technology (eg catalytic systems, aircraft types), driving behaviour (travel speeds, occupancy rates), composition of the vehicle fleet, the primary energy sources used for electricity production (eg oil, gas) and existing environmental standards. Future forecasts are based on the assumption that the now best available techniques will be generally applied by the year 2010 and that more stringent environmental standards will be imposed for passenger cars and aircraft, as well as for power plants and refineries.

The initial aim of the study was to calculate impacts at the European level. All impacts were first calculated for the lowest feasible level, ie per section of the network or on a national scale, taking into account national characteristics where possible, and then aggregated for the 14 countries.

Comparisons between modes and scenarios are based on estimates of total impact (ie in absolute numbers), and of the relative impact (ie impact per passenger-kilometre). Because of the many uncertainties and assumptions underlying the future forecasts, which inevitably involved a fair degree of 'expert judgement', the impact quantifications can only be seen as orders of magnitudes. This was not, however, perceived as a problem, since the analysis of results mainly focused on the comparison between scenarios, rather than on the absolute magnitude of the impacts.

The study results were analysed in the light of the environmental and mobility objectives and targets that are formulated in the Fifth Environmental Action Programme and the Common Transport Policy.

Baseline Data

Where possible, use was made of existing European databases (eg the CORINAIR database on emission factors). However, for most aspects, such databases proved to be either absent or incomplete. The most time-consuming task in the SEA was therefore the collection and harmonisation of data from 14 countries, each with very different registration systems. Another major difficulty was the difference in data availability between the modes: the environmental impact of road traffic is much more studied and documented than the impact of air and rail traffic.

The data collection was mainly achieved through an extensive survey of international institutions, national ministries of transport and environment, research centres, industry, NGOs and consultancies. Additional information was obtained from an international review of EISs of existing HSR projects.

Main Findings of the SEA

The overall study results are presented in Tables 6.1 and 6.2. For certain aspects, the HSR network can certainly make a positive contribution to the lowering of the environmental impact of long-distance transport, and thus to the development of a sustainable transport system. The benefits of the 2010 HST scenario are most clearly demonstrated for quantifiable aspects, and mainly involve the lowering of energy consumption and carbon dioxide emissions, the reduction of air pollution and an overall increase in traffic safety.

All the same, construction of the HSR infrastructure and implementation of technical measures and standard setting will not suffice to realise the EU's environmental targets, such as the reduction of energy consumption and carbon dioxide emissions (see Figure 6.2). Additional measures should be envisaged to reduce the drastic growth of road traffic and to encourage the switch to more environmentally friendly modes and collective transport such as rail. There is a growing consensus that this can in part be achieved by the full integration of external costs into the transport pricing system.

One of the impacts of the network that is generally perceived as negative is the extra hectares of land take it entails. The network requires a total land use of about 80,000 hectares, 40 per cent of which is completely new land use needed for the construction of new HSR lines, and 15 per cent is extra land used for the upgrading of lines. The remaining 45 per cent is taken up by existing infrastruc-

Table 6.1 *Estimtes of Environmental Impacts: 1988 and 2010 HST*

	Units	1988 Road	Air	Rail	Total	2010 HST Road	Air	Rail	Total
Traffic flows	billion pkm	443.3	71.69	92.39	607.4	563.7	126.0	234.1	923.8
Environmental impact									
Land use	1000 ha	282.3	41.67	63.01	387.01	290.8	44.08	80.38	415.23
Primary energy consumption	PJ	855	183	71	1109	959	272	173	1404
Emissions CO	kt	1577	41.32	1.29	1620	713	63.78	0.80	778
NO_x	kt477	66.35	15.81	559	144	87.71	22.57	254	84
HC	kt	180	22.5	0.64	203	54	30.09	0.26	
CO_2	1000 kt	54.04	13.37	3.00	70.41	62.57	19.90	6.46	88.93
SO_2	kt	31.97	4.26	10.54	46.77	17.03	6.34	24.17	47.54
PM	kt	3.99	1.03	1.79	6.81	5.64	1.55	4.89	12.08
acid equivalents	1000 kt	11.50	1.59	0.675	13.76	3.69	2.13	1.25	7.06
CO equivalents	1000 kt	249.27	25.09	4.72	279.1	75.85	33.44	7.55	116.9
Unsafety No of fatalities		2866	29	63	2958	2890	44	71	3005

Source: Mens en Ruimte, 1993

Table 6.2 *Estimates of Environmental Impacts: Difference Between Scenarios*

Impact	Units	2010 HST – 1988		2010 HST – 2010 REF		2010 HST – 2010 FM	
		Total	Per cent of 1988	Total	Per cent of 2010 REF	Total	Per cent of 2010 FM
Land use (2)			-7%				
Primary energy consumption (3)	PJ	295	+27%	-64	-4%	-107	
Emissions CO	kt	-842	-52%	-63	-7%	-87	-10%
NO_x	kt	-305	-55%	-18	-7%	-26	-9%
HC	kt	-119	-59%	-15	-15%	-19	-18%
CO_2	1000 kt	18.52	+26%	-6.75	-7%	-9.56	-10%
SO_2	kt	0.77	+2%	7.00	+18%	6.00	+15%
PM	kt	5.19	+76%	1.00	+9%	1.00	+9%
acid equivalents	1000 kt	-6.70	-50%	-0.18	-2.5%	-0.39	-5%
CO equivalents	1000 kt	-162.2	-60%	-11.75	-9%	-15.55	-12%
Unsafety No of fatalities	No of fatalities	47	+2%	-232	-7%	-308	-9%

1 This table only summarizes those aspects which can be quantified.

2 The sections in the 2010 motorway network not operational in 1988 have for 1988 been replaced by parallel roads with 2x1 lanes, hence the difference in land use for the present and future road network. The differences in land use are not included because the HST network has different locations than the classic rail network. The land use for the 2010 FM scenario has not been calculated, since this scenario would involve an extension of the road network.

3 Conversion factors: 1 MJ primary energy = 0.0209 kg gasoline
　　　　　　　　　　= 0.0220 kg diesel
　　　　　　　　　　= 0.207 kg LPG
　　　　　　　　　　= 0.2333 kg kerosene
　　　　　　　　　　= 0.1056 kWh electricity

$1 MJ = 10^6 J$
$1 PJ = 10^{15} J$
$1 kt = 1000 tons$

Source: Mens en Ruimte, 1993

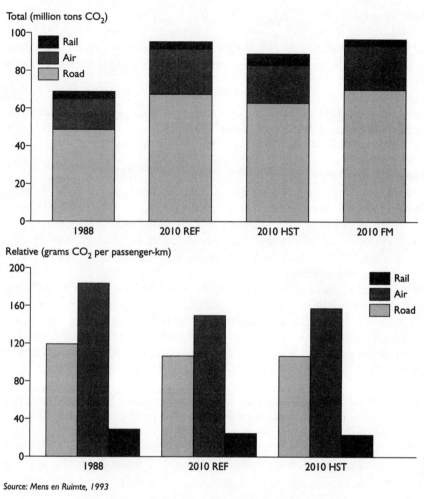

Source: Mens en Ruimte, 1993

Figure 6.2 *Carbon Dioxide (CO₂) Emissions*

ture. The motorway network, on the other hand, consumes more than 3.5 times the surface needed by the HSR network.

Of course, the extra land take by the HSR network is not directly compensated for by the reduction of land use by the other modes. But compared with building new motorways or enlarging airports, HSR offers scope for rational land use, as it uses less space and offers higher capacities than the competing modes of transport. The extent to which the HSR network could solve or mitigate congestion problems by changing the modal split of intercity traffic is, however, not yet clear. A rough estimate showed that the reduction of traffic intensities on motorways following the introduction of the HSR would not solve problems on heavily congested motorway sections, especially because regional traffic and freight traffic would remain unaffected. Airports would, however, benefit more from a changing modal split. Since the number of intra-European flights would be reduced considerably, extra 'slots' would become available for other commercial traffic.

The visual and barrier effect of HSR lines can be severe because of the overhead infrastructure and the fact that the lines are fenced in (for safety reasons and to keep animals off the tracks). The HST's large turning circle also often makes it difficult to avoid sensitive sites. At the time of the study, the databases on land cover and biotopes that were developed within the CORINE program were far from complete, which rendered a quantitative analysis of the network's impact on natural habitats impossible. A first and crucial step in the future SEA process should therefore be to define and identify valuable landscapes and sensitive sites, and to assign them a protection classification. As a minimum requirement, planning of the network should take account of existing protected areas, such as those regulated by the Habitats Directive (EEC 92/43) that came into force in 1995.

Noise, being a local effect, also proved to be a particularly difficult aspect to assess at this strategic level. Rough calculations of noise contours suggest that the reduction of the number of trips by passenger cars following the implementation of the HSR network will only result in a slight reduction in nuisance noise caused by motorways. For nuisance noise around airports, the HSR will have a clearer beneficial effect. At the same speed, an HST running on upgraded lines makes less noise than a conventional train, owing to the technological advances built into it. When operating at higher speeds and greater frequency, the HST produces more noise than conventional trains. If no noise abatement measures are taken, this will entail an increase in nuisance. However, current practice (eg the French HSR lines) shows that noise abatement measures will be an integral part of the planning and construction of new HSR lines and the upgrading of existing lines.

Dissemination of Results, Public Consultation and the SEA's Role in Decision-Making

The overall SEA results were presented in a final report, and in five annexes which detailed the findings for each impact. The report was given only limited distribution by the Commission and is only made available on request. Even though the distribution of the final report is restricted, it has been thoroughly discussed and reviewed by the relevant departments of the DGVII and DGXI, the High Level Group and also by the various interested parties (mainly from road, air and rail industries and organisations).

An executive summary of the SEA was published by the Commission and distributed widely (CEC, 1993b). In addition, in early 1995 a summary of the results was included in the High Level Group's second report on HSR, together with an overview of the results of the studies on traffic evolution and socioeconomic effects.

Apart from the international survey conducted by the consultant, no NGOs were involved in the official procedure, nor was a formal public consultation process conducted. Even though environmental protection groups have expressed their concerns regarding the environmental implications of the network (eg T&E, 1995; Greenpeace, 1995), no clear strategy to address these concerns has been developed.

As far as can be established, the SEA has had no significant influence in the decision-making process on the network, except for demonstrating that HSR is – for most aspects – a more environmentally friendly mode. Since 1990, the network has been modified, but it is not clear what role environmental considerations played in the decision to modify. One of the major problems in assessing the role of the SEA in the decision-making process is that no trade-off analysis was ever made between environmental effects, socioeconomic effects and investment implications.

Further Developments and Recommendations

The main merit of the SEA pilot study on the HSR network is that it proves that SEA can be successfully applied from a very early stage in the decision-making process and – more important – that existing methods and tools can be successfully applied to the SEA of the TEN, especially if further efforts are made to develop the necessary databases. At present, it is not clear whether the Commission still intends to assess the multimodal TEN as a whole, or whether it will opt for a corridor approach. In either case, building on the experience of the HSR study, the following recommendations can be made.

Development of Integrated Databases

The HSR study was conducted by a team of approximately five experts, over a time span of about ten months, and took about 40 person-months. More than half of this time was spent gathering data about the different countries and modes. One of the main recommendations of the study is therefore that the further development of harmonised databases for Europe (including traffic, environmental, economic and demographic data) is necessary. The European Environment Agency should play a significant role in this. If such databases were available, the time needed for SEA could be reduced to approximately five months, thus making SEA a much more acceptable and flexible tool.

Optimising Methods and Models

To guarantee that environmental considerations are fully integrated in the decision making process, the SEA needs to be considered on the same level as financial considerations and socioeconomic evaluations. This requires the development of an integrated assessment method and model, which would allow analysis of trade-offs between environmental impacts, socioeconomic effects and investment considerations. If these links are not established, SEA risks remaining very much a pro-forma exercise.

The need for this integrated approach was already expressed in the White Paper in 1992. Research in this area has, amongst others, been conducted in the Commission's EURET and COST programmes, and further in-depth research will be conducted in the fourth research and development programme. In an ongoing DGVII study, guidelines and recommendations regarding the scope, methodology, tools and data requirements for the SEA of the TEN are being developed; the results of this study are expected at the end of 1995. Another study for DGXI is investigating the issue of traffic induced by new transport infrastructure. However, notwithstanding these many research efforts, progress to date has been very slow. Especially in the light of the year 2010 'deadline', it seems advisable to opt for a more pragmatic 'KISS' (keep it simple and start) approach.

In the HSR study, the use of geographic information systems (GIS) was limited mostly to the calculation of land-take. However, in the future SEA of the TEN or its corridors, GIS will certainly be used as an important analysis tool. Particularly for the assessment of noise nuisance and the impact on landscapes and sensitive sites, GIS zoning and overlay modules can provide interesting solutions, provided again that an effort is made to develop the necessary underlying data. An interesting study in this regard has recently been published by the Royal Society for the Protection of Birds (1995), in which a GIS was developed to analyse the impact of the road network on bird habitats. Another example of a GIS-oriented approach is the multimodal SEA of the French northern corridor that was conducted for the French ministry of environment (Ministère de l'Environnement, 1994). This study compares the environmental sensitivity profiles of the region (or its carrying capacity) against the environmental impact of the different modes.

Procedure

Apart from the development of SEA methodologies, setting up a clear SEA procedure is of prime importance. A first issue to be clarified is the responsibility of the European Commission (DGVII and DGXI) and the member states in regard to the SEA of the TENs. So far, it is unclear to what extent the results of a Community-level SEA can be binding on the member states, and what the SEA's link to national-level SEAs and EIA at the project level would be. This situation is exacerbated by the fact that the results of SEAs conducted on an EU level are at present not considered to be a condition for Commission funding. This legal and procedural situation regarding SEA should be clarified in the guidelines when they are finally agreed by the European Parliament and the Council of Ministers.

Public consultation remains another important issue. The White Paper recognised that improvement of the environmental performance of the Community's transport systems requires the participation of all actors. So far, however, the political discussion on the TEN has mostly been conducted between the Community's institutions, national and regional authorities, industry and transport operators. A strategy should also be developed to address concerns that are increasingly being expressed by transport users, environmental protection groups and local authorities (T&E, 1995). Of course, this means that a proper balance needs to be struck between confidentiality requirements, which can be very stringent at the strategic levels of decision-making, and public consultation needs.

SEA of the Community Transport Policy?

The Community's transport policy seems to be very much geared towards the objective of increasing mobility which, primarily for socioeconomic reasons, is considered to be a desirable goal. It is, however, doubtful whether continuous growth in mobility can be compatible with sustainability objectives, especially if this growth continues to be mainly realised by road transport, as many studies predict.

Apart from the development of the TEN, the White Paper outlined a number of other priority actions aimed at promoting the use of environmentally friendly transport modes and collective transport. It therefore seems advisable to assess the TEN in the wider framework of all proposed community transport policy measures and priority actions. Ideally, the future SEA of the TEN should include various policy scenarios, in which not only the effects of alternative transport networks and corridors but also of traffic demand management, pricing and regulatory measures can be assessed and subjected to sensitivity analysis.

7
SEA of the Dutch Ten-Year Programme on Waste Management 1992–2002

Rob Verheem

Introduction

The Dutch Waste Management Council (WMC) developed its Ten-Year Programme on Waste Management 1992–2002 (TYP 92) in 1992. This programme plans and coordinates the technology and capacity needed for final waste processing in the next ten years in the Netherlands. This case study describes the SEA that was carried out in developing this programme, focusing on the scenarios and alternatives that were developed and the methodology that was used to assess the environmental impacts of these alternatives. The success of this SEA and the review of its quality by the independent Dutch EIA Commission is discussed briefly.

Institutional Framework and SEA Procedure

Institutional Framework

The WMC was established in 1990 as a joint agreement between the Ministry of the Environment, the Association of Provincial Authorities, and the Association of the Dutch Municipalities. Its purpose is to plan and coordinate waste management at the national level, thus ensuring an efficient approach. The actual management of waste treatment and processing is carried out by the members of the WMC.

Table 7.1 *Amounts of Waste (in Kilotons) to be Finally Processed: Present and Future Situation*

Type of waste	Present situation (year 1990)	Policy scenario (year 2000)	Headwind scenario (year 2000)
Normal domestic waste	4680	2203	3532
Coarse domestic waste	540	438	470
Commercial waste	1480	781	1092
Industrial waste	2810	2267	2777
Sewage sludge	1120	776	885
Clinical waste	120	72	96
Construction and demolition waste	3500	1996	4006
Shredder waste (car wrecks)	120	136	153
Separate vegetable and garden waste	280	2634	2151
Total	14,650	11,303	15,162

Source: WMC, 1992b

Once every three years the WMC draws up a TYP on waste management to plan the technology and capacities needed for the final treatment of a number of waste flows:

- domestic waste;
- industrial waste;
- construction and demolition waste;
- commercial waste (from offices, shops and services);
- sewage sludge;
- shredder waste (processed car wrecks); and
- clinical (hospital) waste.

Planning actions to prevent or re-use waste are outside the scope of the TYP.

The ten-year programme provides the framework for the provincial waste management plans, in which final decisions are taken on the methods and capacities of waste processing. Because final decisions are taken at the provincial level, an SEA is compulsory for the provincial waste management plans only; for the national programme an SEA is carried out voluntarily.

The SEAs for both types of plans are 'tiered' as much as possible to prevent overlap. In practice this means that planning and environmental assessment are tiered along the following lines:

- At the national level decisions are taken regarding principal choices for final waste treatment, eg dumping versus incineration, and the total processing capacities needed. In the SEA, available options are identified and their impacts assessed.
- At the provincial level final decisions are taken regarding locations at which processing should take place, the methods to be used at each location and the capacities needed for each of these methods. The SEA assesses the environmental consequences of the use of alternative locations and the effects of waste processing at these locations.
- At the project level, at each of the selected locations design and mitigation measures are decided, inter alia, on the basis of a project EIA.

SEA Procedure

While preparing the TYP 92, the WMC decided to carry out an SEA of the programme on a voluntary basis. However, in the Netherlands a voluntary EIA is only possible if it is carried out in full compliance with the existing EA regulations. Therefore, the SEA procedure for TYP 92 was exactly the same as those for projects and plans that require EA. This means, for example, that the procedure included the following steps:

- the publication of a 'starting note' which, inter alia, describes the purpose and objectives of the TYP, gives a first overview of possible alternatives and indicates impacts to be expected;
- a scoping process, including full consultation of the environmental authorities and the general public, as well as the independent scoping advice of the Dutch EIA Commission;
- preparation of an environmental impact statement (EIS), including a description of alternatives, amongst which is an 'alternative best for the environment';
- a review process, again including full consultation and the independent reviewing advice of the EIA Commission.

In light of the strategic character of the programme, the WMC also decided to fully participate in the preparation of the waste management programmes and the SEAs of all the regional and local authorities that would be responsible for implementing the national programme (VROM, 1992).

Methodology Used in the SEA

Scenarios for the Production of Waste

As a basis for the development of alternatives for the programming of final

Table 7.2 *Alternative Options to Final Waste Processing (in Kilotons): Policy Scenario**

Method by which waste is finally processed	Intended programme	Reference programme	Alt I	Alt II	Alt III
To be incinerated:					
Integral waste**	3972	5117	2625	0	0
High calorific waste (dry fraction)	782	0	75	3568	1825
Residual waste	361	274	0	652	0
To be landfilled:					
Integral waste**	0	0	2376	0	0
Non-combustible	3698	3552	3574	4157	4157
High calorific waste (dry fraction)	0	0	0	0	1743
Residual waste	398	409	548	359	896
To be composted:					
Unpolluted organic material	1170	1170	1170	1170	1170
Polluted organic material	901	684	703	0	0
To be digested:					
Unpolluted organic material	780	780	780	780	780
Polluted organic material	0	0	0	1628	1628
To be collected separately:					
Unpolluted organic material	1950	1950	1950	1950	1950
Polluted organic material	684	684	684	684	684

*This table shows the total amounts of waste to be dealt with, based on the 'policy scenario' for future waste production. In the EIS a similar table is given based on the amounts of waste to be expected in the 'head-wind scenario'.
** All kinds of waste mixed together.

Source: WMC, 1992a

waste disposal capacity, two scenarios for the development of waste production to be expected in the future were developed (WMC, 1992a): the 'policy scenario' and the 'headwind scenario'. The policy scenario assumed that national objectives regarding waste prevention, reduction, separation, quality improvement and producer/consumer responsibility, as set out in legislation and

Table 7.3 *Summary of the Environmental Effects of Alternative Options: Policy Scenario[a]*

Indicator	Existing situation 1990 — emphasis on landfilling	Intended programme 2000 — pre-separation; incineration of combustible waste	Reference programme 2000 — no pre-separation; incineration of combustible waste	Alt I 2000 — pre-separation; emphasis on landfilling	Alt II 2000 — maximal pre-separation; incineration of combustible waste	Alt III 2000 — maximal pre-separation; emphasis on landfilling
Dispersion of toxins:						
Hg and Cd (kg)	5457	5445	5696	3257	4632	2463
PACs[b] (kg)	62	3.7	3.8	3.1	3.4	2.7
dioxins (g)	147	4.1	4.3	2.2	3.3	1.5
organic substances (t)	792	202	211	359	228	303
Acidification: SO_2						
and NO_x (Meq H[c]).	222	107	111	68	99	53
Disturbance: odour (10^{12} ge[d])	17	55	43	45	9	9
Climatic change:						
CO_2 and CH_4 (kton[e])	4349	−1496	−1525	−175	−1526	−494
Energy use (PJ)	6.2	20.9	21.5	11.4	20.1	−9.6
Production of residuals:						
res. to be landfilled (kton)	220	398	402	548	359	896
chemical waste (kton)	118	164	164	76	165	49
res. to be recovered (kton)	637	1802	1891	1316	1502	1043
Space occupied (ha)	79	29	28	46	32	50

[a] This table is based on the 'policy scenario' for future waste production. The EIS contains a similar table based on the 'head-wind scenario'; [b] poly-aromatic carbon hydroxides; [c] mass equivalent hydrogen: acid equivalents; [d] odour units; [e] CO_2 equivalents

Source: WMC, 1992b

national environmental management plans, would be fully achieved. It also assumed that future European waste management policy would be in line with policies established in north-western European countries. The headwind scenario assumed that these objectives would not be fully achieved, and that therefore more waste would have to be dealt with. Table 7.1 indicates the amounts of different types of waste to be expected (and thus that would need processing) in the future, following both scenarios. As a reference, the amounts of waste produced in the existing situation are given.

The Intended Programme and Alternative Options

In the existing situation (1990), approximately 75 per cent of the waste in the Netherlands was (finally) landfilled, 20 per cent was incinerated and the rest was re-used. The decision about which disposal method to use depended mainly on the availability of processing facilities; the composition and nature of the waste was not really taken into consideration. The WMC intended to change this approach in the future, and to shift the focus of final waste processing from landfilling to incineration. The 'intended programme' to process waste in the next ten years, as described in the SEA, was therefore to:

• maintain existing and planned capacity for the pre-separation of waste into a wet fraction (mainly organic) and a dry fraction (mainly inorganic);
• collect and process vegetable, fruit and garden waste separately: 60 per cent to be turned into compost and 40 per cent to be digested;
• incinerate all combustible waste: landfilling of this waste will be forbidden; and
• landfill all non-combustible waste.

The SEA investigated three alternatives to the intended programme. In alternative I the existing situation remains more or less unchanged in the future:

• no capacity expansion for pre-separation of waste;
• no expansion of existing incineration capacity;
• landfilling of remaining waste.

The main objective of alternative II is to pre-separate as much as possible, after which each type of remaining waste is processed according to its nature:

• maximal pre-processing through dry or wet separation;
• digestion of the remaining organic fraction, after which the residues of digestion will be incinerated;
• incineration of all combustible, non-organic waste;
• landfilling of all non-combustible, non-organic waste.

Alternative III is also based on maximal pre-separation, but assumes that there will be no expansion of incineration capacity, and that remaining fractions will be landfilled:

• maximal pre-processing through wet or dry separation;
• digestion of the remaining organic fraction, and landfilling of the residues of digestion;
• landfilling of all the remaining non-organic fraction (both combustible and non-combustible material), with no expansion of incineration.

In principle, it would be possible in the future to incinerate all combustible waste integrally, without any pre-separation. In the SEA this is not regarded an 'alternative' to the intended programme, since it is unlikely to be a feasible or even desirable option for the future. However, an impact assessment of this approach was judged as being potentially valuable for decision-makers, as a reference point against which the real alternatives could be compared. Therefore, this approach is described in the EIS as the reference programme.

Table 7.2 gives a more detailed overview of the alternative options for the waste management programme. For each type of waste it describes which quantities should be processed by which method.

Impact Assessment

To assess the impacts of the alternatives, a method was chosen in which a number of indicators represent certain environmental issues (WMC, 1992b). The EIS discusses how each alternative affects the indicators chosen. The environmental issues were based on the issues mentioned in the Dutch National Environmental Policy Programme:

• dispersion of toxic materials in the environment;
• acidification;
• disturbance (eg noise, smell);
• climatic change;
• use of energy;
• production of residuals; and
• use of space.

Table 7.3 shows the indicators used for each of the issues, and summarises the results of the impact prediction for each indicator and alternative. In addition to these tables, the EIS also shows the results for each indicator in a graph.

Comparing the Alternatives

The SEA used these tables and graphs to compare the environmental impact of the alternatives. No further aggregation or weighting of data took place. Although beforehand it was thought that alternative III would turn out to be the most environmentally friendly alternative, on the basis of this comparison the SEA concluded that alternative II should probably be regarded as such. However, this alternative would require considerable expansion of existing pre-separation and digestion capacity, and therefore was not regarded as feasible in the short term (WMC, 1992b).

The SEA concluded that, for the planning period, from an environmental viewpoint the intended programme was a good compromise between feasibility, reasonable impact on the environment and compatibility with existing environmental policy objectives. This option would lead to a high energy yield, a positive contribution to carbon dioxide reduction and few space requirements. However, the SEA also showed that this approach scores poorly as regards acidification and dispersal of toxic materials, and will lead to relatively large quantities of chemical residuals.

Discussion

Procedure

The early consultation of the general public, and the involvement of the environmental authorities and the independent Dutch EIA Commission, contributed to the quality of the SEA, which is regarded as good (see below). The SEA did not delay the planning process: preparation of the EIS took five months, and the whole SEA procedure took approximately ten months. From the fact that the developer of the programme decided – again on a voluntary basis – to carry out an SEA for the new TYP 1995–2005, one can also conclude that the SEA was regarded as useful by the developer.

The full participation of the regional and local authorities in the SEA led to a broad acceptance of the SEA results and the conclusions in the programme. The SEA could not have been prepared in such a short time without the valuable practical information brought into the process by these authorities.

EIS Quality

The Dutch EIA Commission (EIA Commission, 1992) concluded in its reviewing advice that the EIS generally gives a comprehensive view of the potential environmental impacts of the described alternatives. The use of indicators for a number of environmental issues was judged to be a clear and 'refreshing' methodology which gives a good, although rough, insight into the differences between the impacts of alternatives.

However, there was also some criticism. The 'headwind scenario' was felt to not truly represent a worst-case scenario, since in this scenario the total amount of waste to be finally processed in 2002 was less than that in 1990: this might not be realistic in a scenario that is supposed to be pessimistic. Furthermore, it was not clear to the commission why the technique of waste 'digestion' was part of some alternatives, whilst other techniques that are equally new and uncertain (such as the gasification of waste) were not; it would have been more consistent if techniques that are still uncertain were part of either all or none of the alternatives.

The commission queried why particular indicators for the dispersion of toxic materials in the environment were chosen, and felt that odour-hindrance had been underestimated. It also criticised the fact that in the comparison between alternatives no weighting of the relative importance of impacts had taken place in light of the total environmental problems in the Netherlands. This may lead to wrong conclusions. For example, the differences between the alternatives' scores on the climatic change indicator are totally irrelevant in light of the total existing carbon dioxide and methane production in the Netherlands, whilst the differences in dioxin production are very relevant, since waste incineration is one of the main contributors to this type of pollution.

8
SEA of the Bara Forest Management Plan, Nepal

Ram Khadka, John McEachern, Olavi Rautiainen, and Uttam S Shrestha

Introduction

The Kingdom of Nepal extends for about 800 kilometres along the Himalayas and has a population of 19 million. Thirty-seven per cent of Nepal is covered by natural forests. The major tree species in Nepal's forests are sal *(Shorea robusta)* in the tropics and sub-tropics, fir in the high Himal, chirpine and oak in the mid-mountains, and blue pine in the high mountains and mid-mountains. Forests provide 75 per cent of domestic energy and 40 per cent of livestock nutrition, and contribute about 15 per cent to the national gross domestic product (HMG et al, 1988).

A large part of the forest in the lowlands of Nepal (Terai) has been destroyed as part of the area's conversion into agricultural land by people who have migrated from the mountains since the late 1950s. About 100,000 hectares of Terai forest were deforested for settlement purposes between 1950 and 1985. More forest areas were destroyed due to unregulated extraction, periodic political chaos, frequent floods, erosion and massive illicit timber felling by the local people. Between 1965 and 1979, the annual rate of forest depletion was as high as 25 per cent (Parajuli, 1994).

Past government policies such as the Forest Nationalisation Act of 1957 aimed to promote the country's economy by collecting revenue from forest resources. The Forest Act of 1961, its amendment in 1970 and the National Forest Plan of 1976 set out some provisions for developing community forestry, and this initiative was supported by the Decentralisation Act of 1982. However, due to the unsatisfactory effect of these acts and policies, the government formulated a long-term Master Plan for the Forestry Sector (MPFS) in 1989, with a view to improving the condition of Nepal's forests. The Eighth Five-Year Plan (1992–1997) and the Forestry Sector Act of 1993 supported the plan and activities proposed in the MPFS; however, the current act does not provide any direction or provisions for institutional reform, and this has become an obstacle to implementing the MPFS (Parajuli, 1994). In response to the MPFS, Nepal's Department of Forestry, in collaboration with the Forest Management Utilisation Development Project, developed a production-oriented Operational Forest Management Plan (OFMP) to be implemented on a pilot scale in the Bara District forest (see Figure 8.1) (Seppanen and Acharya, 1994).

This chapter discusses the findings of an SEA carried out for the OFMP. It begins with a discussion of the OFMP and explains why the SEA was undertaken, then reviews the various stages of the SEA: baseline information, impact prediction and evaluation, mitigation and monitoring. It concludes with a discussion of proposed changes to the OFMP.

The Proposed Operational Forest Management Plan

The OFMP for the Bara District forest aims to implement production-oriented forest activities in order to meet the increasing demand for forest products and to improve Nepal's economy. It shifts emphasis from protection forestry to production-oriented forest management, particularly for sal. The reasons for doing this were that:

- natural sal forests are disappearing exceedingly rapidly in Nepal, while the demand for sal timber is increasing, nationally and internationally (Kanel, 1994);
- past practices of allowing the contractor to harvest only mature trees and current practices of allowing people to collect only dead and decayed forest products, has left 80–85 per cent of overmature, inferior-quality trees. Such a 'slum forest' needs to be replaced by regenerating forest (Pesonen, 1994); and
- regeneration felling will open up the forest floor so that sal saplings can find sufficient light to grow (Rautiainen, 1994).

The proposed OFMP aims to achieve higher volumes of timber and fuel wood production on a sustainable basis, higher revenues to local and national government, increased employment opportunities for local people, reduced levels of environmental and forest degradation, and reduced poaching of timber and wildlife.

For the implementation of OFMP, the Bara District forest is divided into production forests, potential community and leasehold forests, and protection

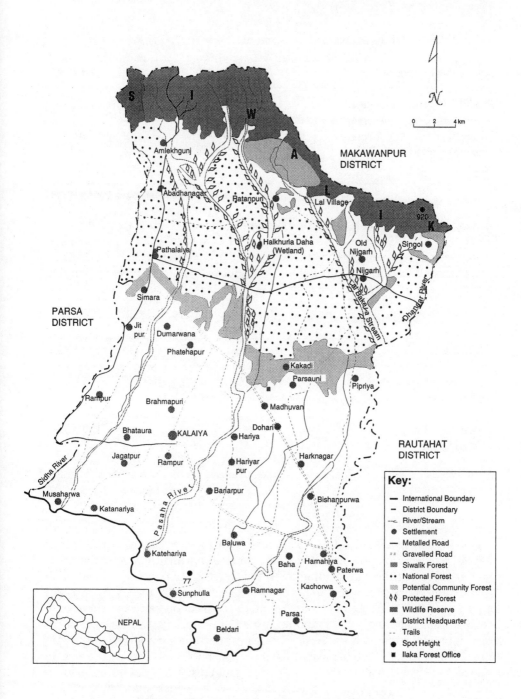

Figure 8.1 *Land Uses in the Bara District, Nepal*

Table 8.1 *Forest Area and Management Categories: Bara District Forest*

Management category	Area (ha)	Per cent
Production forest: even-aged	24,298.5	75
Production forest: uneven-aged	1660.6	5
Potential community forest	3197.4	10
Protection forest	3273.8	10
Total	32,430.3	100

Source: Seppanen and Acharya, 1994

forests, as shown in Table 8.1. The existing structure of Bara Forest is shown in Table 8.2. The OFMP proposes that a total forest area of 1830 hectares should be harvested between 1994–5 and 1998–9 by using different harvesting practices (Figure 8.2). This would yield forest products of different types, generating a government revenue of more than 500 million Nepalese rupees (Table 8.3).

Table 8.2 *Development Class Structure: Bara District Forest*

Forest structure	Per cent	Volume (m³/ha)
Open area, regeneration area	0	0
Sapling forest	1	31
Pole forest	3	74
Middle-aged forest	44	169
Mature forest	52	168
Total	100	165

Source: Seppanen and Acharya, 1994

Since the majority of trees in the Bara District forest belong to the light-demanding, dominant species of sal, the plan targets this species, relying heavily on its natural regeneration potential. The forest comprises primarily mature and overmature trees, with few developing trees, thus regeneration felling, ie harvesting mature and overmature trees, is crucial to ensuring a fully stocked second generation of forest. Fire and grazing are the most common causes of damage to regenerating seedlings of sal, and are usually human induced, so to gain co-operation and support from local people in protecting the regenerating forest, the OFMP includes employment of local people at 3000 jobs per year. The plan also allows local people to collect dead, dying and diseased trees from the forest for domestic use (Seppanen and Acharya, 1994). It proposes that environmentally sensitive areas, such as the foothills of the Siwalik range, Halkhuriya Lake, and 100-metre buffer zones on either side of major rivers should be left intact as

Table 8.3 *Area to be Harvested, Yield and Revenues*

Harvesting pratice	Area to be harvested	Yield (m³/ha)	Revenue (000 NRs)
Immature thinning[a]	583.5	11,510	4048
Seedling felling[b]	114.9	50,570	7860
Regeneration felling[c]	1060.0	215,350	501,958
Selection felling[d]	71.7	2860	4368

a First thinning maintains 1700 trees/ha; second maintains 110 trees/ha.
b Most large canopy trees harvested, exposing seedlings to light but still retains 110–130 large stems.
c Like clear felling, but some matured trees left for seeding.
d Logs and firewood harvested while maintaining uneven-aged structure.

Source: Seppanen and Acharya, 1994

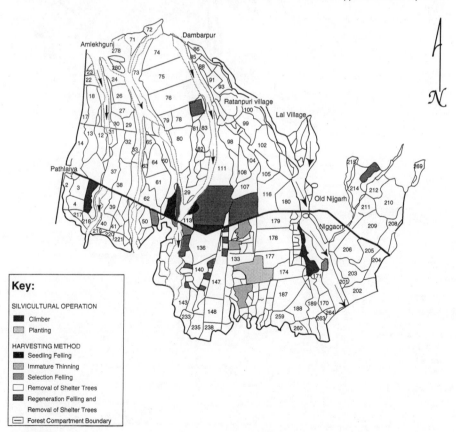

Figure 8.2 *Areas Proposed for Harvesting and Silviculture in the First Five Years*

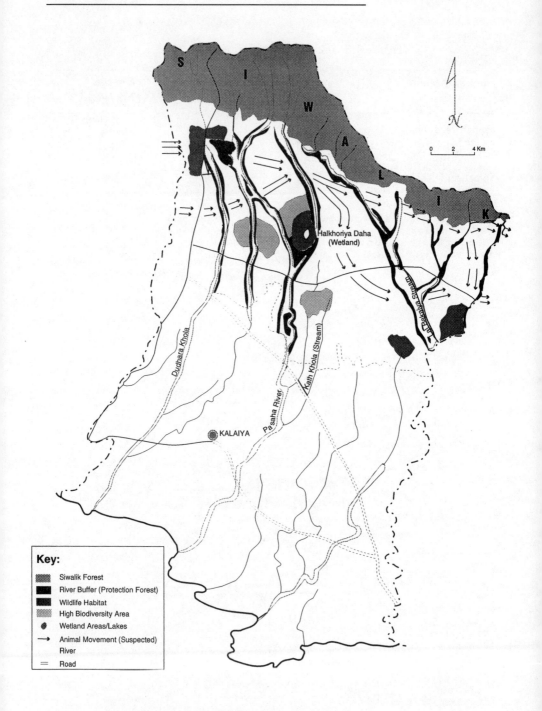

Figure 8.3 *Environmentally Sensitive Areas in the Bara District, Nepal*

protected forest (Figure 8.3). The OFMP is being proposed for implementation on an experimental basis on 18,000 hectares in the first five years, and 26,000 hectares per year thereafter.

The Reasons for Undertaking an SEA

Implementing a forest management plan like the OFMP for Bara District includes activities for shifting from one type of management to another, and will cause an array of adverse and beneficial impacts associated with the bio-physical, social and economic aspects of the area. It is thus important to analyse the consequences of implementing such management plans on environmental grounds, so that predicted negative consequences can be avoided or minimised by considering alternatives and adopting appropriate cost-effective mitigation measures (IUCN/Nepal, 1995; Wood, 1988). Integration of EA at a strategic level helps to refine the proposed plan so that environmental issues are properly accounted for, and the plan's benefits are achieved in a sustainable manner.

Environmental assessment in Nepal is still in its infancy. However, the national guidelines on EIA (HMG, 1994) and the sectoral EIA guidelines for the forestry sector (NPC et al, 1993) require forestry management plans to undergo SEA. As such, the Nepalese Department of Forestry and the Forest Management Utilisation Development Project officially requested IUCN/Nepal to carry out an SEA for the OFMP.

IUCN/Nepal coordinated a task force of consultants who collected baseline information on various aspects related to the OFMP. Impacts examined in the SEA included those on:

- the existing natural environment;
- the people living in Bara District who might be affected;
- the economy of Bara District and its potential contribution to the national economy under a different management regime; and
- the institutional context affecting the proposal and its implementation.

Individual consultant reports were analysed and discussed in a series of workshops. These baseline data were then used in making predictions about the magnitude, extent and duration of the OFMP's likely impacts.

Because the SEA of the OFMP for Bara District is the first of its kind in Nepal, baseline data are incomplete in many aspects. It was not possible to assess a wide array of alternatives in the absence of adequate data. Therefore, two main alternatives were assessed. The first, 'do-nothing' alternative refers to what would happen if the current situation continues. The second alternative refers to the conditions likely to occur when the proposed management regime is implemented. A list of positive and negative impacts was drawn up for each alternative, and through a process of discussions and consensus building, the magnitude, extent and duration of each impact was determined. Negative impacts associated with the first alternative would be reduced or even eliminated by the second alternative. However, implementation of the second alternative would create a new series of impacts, and these similarly must be assessed.

The final analysis must determine if the benefits associated with the second alternative are sufficient to outweigh the negative factors. In this context, the analysis must include a degree of certainty, since changing the status quo makes little sense if the likelihood of actual benefits is small (IUCN/Nepal, 1995).

Baseline Information

Project Location and Physiography (Figure 8.1)
Bara District is located 200 kilometres south of the capital Kathmandu and lies at an average elevation of 150–200 metres as an extension of the Indo-Gangetic Plain (Terai). Geological formations include tertiary materials in the north and alluvial plains in the south. The area is hot with a wet, sub-tropical monsoon and tropical dry temperature in winter (Seppanen and Acharya, 1994).

Flora (Figure 8.1)
The Bara forest consists of 8 per cent forest dominated by monotypic stands of sal, 68 per cent Terai mixed-hardwood forest comprising mainly sal and its associates, 12 per cent Khair-sisso forest along river banks and 12 per cent degraded forest. Endangered, rare and indigenous plant species include *Acacia concinna*, *Asparagus recemosus* and *Rhamnu nepalensis*, and over 40 species of medicinal plants are reportedly collected by the local people for herbal medicines (Upreti, 1994).

Fauna
Of the 19 species of endangered mammals listed in the National Park and Wildlife Act of 1973 and CITES Appendix 1985, five – the elephant, four-horned antelope, tiger, wild dog, and clouded leopard – reportedly exist in the area. Animals still currently found in the adjoining Parsa Wildlife Reserve were also believed to exist previously in the Bara forest, but hunting and poaching by local people, coupled with continuous habitat degradation, has led to the decline of wildlife (Uprety, 1994).

Special Sites for Conservation (Figure 8.3)
Halkhuriya Lake, which covers 15 hectares in the middle of the Bara forest, is the only perennial wetland. The lake has religious and cultural value locally, and people also harvest its fish. Wild animals and almost 13,000 cattle use the lake as a source of drinking water (McEachern and Bhandari, 1994).

Population and Sociocultural Aspects (Figure 8.1)
The area contains 415,718 people and 68,952 households, with a heterogeneous socioeconomic and ethnic structure of local communities. The average family size is seven (CBS, 1993). Almost 71 per cent of the total population are employed in agriculture, 5–8 per cent are involved in business and trade, and 10 per cent are landless and live in dire poverty. These people are reportedly involved in illicit felling and smuggling of wood worth NRs 5 million annually (US$1 = approximately 54 NR). Some are also engaged in collecting and selling firewood and medicinal plants from the forest (Koirala, 1994). Tuberculosis, gastric problems, malnutrition and snake bites are the major causes of death. Infant mortality, which is primarily associated with malnourishment, is comparatively high (Manushi, 1994).

There are 302,323 head of livestock, of which 10,000 reportedly graze in the Bara forest daily. No system of stall feeding exists (Koirala, 1994). An average of 140,000 tonnes per year of fuel wood, 115,000 tonnes per year of fodder and 20,000 cubic metres per year of timber are harvested from the Bara forest (Joshi, 1994b).

The Bara forest has been subject to large-scale clearance so that high-ranking bureaucrats, army personnel and relatives, and favourites of royalty could acquire arable lands. There are more than 100 such families who each enjoy 6–25 hectares of agricultural land obtained through special royal command. Most of these lands are within the Bara District forest (Manushi, 1994).

Institutional and Administration Aspects
The Department of Forestry (DoF) develops and supervises plans and programmes, and ensures that the forestry development programmes are implemented. The Forest Management and Silvicultural section assists in the preparation, implementation and supervision of the forest management plans and programmes. The District Forest Office under the DoF has overall responsibility for implementing policies and programmes at the district level and running extension and training programmes, as well as carrying out judicial functions for forest protection (Budhathoki, 1994).

The present organisation for the administration of the district's forest is primarily oriented towards protection. The major gap at present is the heavy load of forest protection activities with insufficient skilled workers. The District Forest Office's lack of authority over the harvesting and sale of forest products indicates mistrust between district offices and central authorities.

An appropriate organisation with highly motivated, skilled and well-trained staff is a paramount requirement for the effective implementation of the proposed OFMP. Special attention should be given to avoiding duplication of work and confusion of roles, responsibilities and authority of the District forest office with the central level. District Forest Offices require expansion and strengthening to effectively implement and monitor the management plan. A fire control officer and support staff are required to protect natural regeneration sites from fire hazards (Budhathoki, 1994).

Predicted Impacts and Their Significance

Approximately 150 impacts were identified on the basis of the consultants' reports. These impacts were then discussed, and their significance analysed, in a series of workshops attended by consultants, NGOs, proponents, stakeholders, policy-makers and forest administrators. The impacts were distilled into 19 broad, generic issues through consensus. These issues were discussed for both alternatives, and ranked by magnitude, extent and duration, following the ranking method shown in Table 8.4. The following are some of the major issues identified, analysed and ranked, in no particular order of importance.

Table 8.4 *Ranking Method**

Magnitude		Extent		Duration	
High/major	60	Regional	60	Long-term	20
Moderate	20	Local	20	Medium-term	10
Minor	10	Site-specific	10	Short-term	5

* Maximum score (for major, regional, long-term impacts) is 140; minimum score (for minor, site-specific, short-term impacts) is 2.5.

Source: HMG, 1994; NPC et al, 1993

Involvement of People Likely to be Affected by Project Implementation
About 10 per cent of people in Bara District are poor and landless, and earn their livelihood through the exploitation of forest resources. They will be affected by the plan's implementation, particularly due to changes in tenure and legislation. The employment of such people in the project is necessary in order to make implementation of the plan successful. The OFMP prescribes involvement of local people, but lacks detailed descriptions of how training, education and awareness-raising activities for such people will be undertaken, and how their involvement will be promoted; it does not show a budget for this issue. A revised OFMP should include these factors.

Uncontrolled Forest Burning
Forest burning is used to clear land for farming and settlement, and sometimes to stimulate the growth of animal forage. The overall significance of this impact is high, since the fire kills regenerating tree saplings and often destroys a large

part of the forest due to fire in the crowns of trees. Therefore, uncontrolled burning needs to be restricted when the second alternative is implemented. The current OFMP needs additional work to outline the use of proposed fire-line works.

Poaching of Timber and Fuel Wood

Illegal logging and sales of wood are major problems and have led to massive deforestation. Approximately NRs 5 million of timber is being smuggled to India from the Bara forest alone. The overall significance of this impact is high. The implementation of the second alternative would probably reduce such impacts by creating jobs worth NRs 10 million per year. However, the current plan does not provide any details and cost implications of employing local people.

Poaching of Wildlife

This is another impact of high significance, since local people supplement their income by the illegal capture and killing of wildlife. If present trends continue, several wildlife species which are now endangered will become extinct in a few years; however, implementation of the second alternative may make poaching more difficult due to the presence of more people keeping watch in the area. The plan recognises that a problem exists but offers no solutions, nor does it discuss the potential impact of a production forestry regime on the area's wildlife habitats.

Fuel Wood Gathering for Domestic Use

Nearly 97 per cent of the people of Bara District use the forest as a source of fuel wood for cooking. Fuel wood is gathered both legally and illegally. Implementation of the second alternative is likely to increase the fuel wood supply for local or regional use. However, a short transition period will occur during the initial phase of project implementation which may create some social and market dislocation problems. The plan fails to address these problems. In the later stage of plan implementation, a continuous supply of fuel wood is ensured as tops and lops created by silviculture practices could be made available.

Clearing the Forest for Agriculture and Settlement

Clearing the forest for agriculture and settlement is a continuous problem, especially along forest edges, which are continually being pushed back. The issue is rated as significant, regional and long-term. If the second alternative was implemented, forest boundaries would be more clearly defined. The establishment of a community forest might stabilise and reduce the loss of forest land due to clearing. Short-term social dislocations can be expected as people seeking to clear land will be prohibited from doing so. This issue was ranked as being of moderate importance, but needs to be addressed in more detail, since it can produce cumulative impacts and has the long-term potential to seriously deplete the land base available for production forestry. If encroachment is not stopped, this reduction in the land base will directly affect revenues.

Employment
At present, there is insufficient opportunity to employ people in the forest, since no formal management regime is in place. Current employment is indirect, such as illegal poaching and the gathering of minor forest products, with a few direct employment activities associated with existing timber management work. If the second alternative were implemented, more jobs would be created both directly in harvesting and silviculture work and indirectly in support of these activities. The number of new jobs available has not been outlined in detail in the OFMP. More work is thus needed to quantify the number of jobs anticipated and to outline where they will be available, and for how long. The cost figures provided in the plan do not indicate whether they include wages, benefits and administrative overheads, so they cannot be analysed.

Grazing of Animals in the Forest
The regenerating forest is reportedly being destroyed by livestock grazing. Once the OFMP is in place, cattle grazing in the forest will be excluded. However, the plan does not describe the measures for exclusion. It should incorporate measures such as encouraging stall feeding, for which silviculture activities would provide fodder after the second alternative is implemented. This issue ranks high in the early stages of plan implementation but becomes moderate at the latter stage.

Soil Erosion
Soil erosion due to human activities is a major problem. The Siwalik Hills in the north are the most erosion-prone area. The OFMP has indicated that the Siwaliks will remain outside the project area. However, activities such as road construction, logging operations and forest harvesting techniques may induce erosion at locations outside the plan area. The current management plan acknowledges this problem but does not evaluate it in enough detail. Silvicultural and management guidelines are needed to provide detailed prescriptions for minimising soil erosion in the project area (Joshi, 1994a).

Loss of Habitats and Biodiversity
Conservation of biodiversity and habitats is a very important issue, both technically and politically. Failure to recognise the problem and effectively deal with it is likely to create political problems in terms of international perceptions about the way Nepal's remaining forests are being managed. However, the second alternative provides an excellent opportunity to implement an effective biodi-

versity conservation programme and to facilitate its integration with a production forestry regime. The OFMP recognises this issue and stresses the need for an 'environmental survey'. This survey should be incorporated into the management plan so that information derived can be effectively incorporated into a biodiversity implementation manual. A well-planned biodiversity implementation manual will enable an optimum mix of production forest with biodiversity conservation. However, this needs more work.

Tenure Rights of Local People

The issue of tenure and the implementation of the community forest as proposed in the OFMP should be a top priority for senior decision-makers. The success of implementing the second alternative depends largely on effective local involvement in community forestry. If the issues of tenure and the rights of the people to use the forest lands are not dealt with effectively, there will be less chance for the production forestry plan to succeed. The importance of this issue is not sufficiently acknowledged in the plan. A new section should be added, outlining the nature of the issue, factors that currently inhibit successful implementation of community forestry and what needs to be done to overcome the problem.

Legal and Institutional Arrangements

The Forestry Sector Act of 1993 appears to be silent on the concept of production forestry. Article 21 of the act empowers the government to prepare and implement an operational plan after approval by the ministry. However, article 68.1 of the act empowers the government to permit the use of any part of the forest for any type of forestry, provided that the proposed development plan is not likely to affect the environment significantly. Therefore, the plan has to show sufficient and convincing grounds and commitments that its implementation will not affect the environment, but rather will improve the existing degraded environment of the Bara forest. The existing institutional arrangements will not be able to handle the implementation and operation of the OFMP. In the long run, some institutional and administrative reform will be needed. The present OFMP does not address this issue sufficiently.

Timber Harvesting Methods

The OFMP provides considerable detail about the forest harvesting activities envisaged, but fails to adequately discuss how these will be implemented to avoid damage. The plan should be amended to include a specific section outlining how the potential negative impacts of timber harvesting will be avoided. A series of harvesting guidelines would be a useful addition, which, if developed as a separate document, could then be used as part of training and awareness programmes.

Economic Activities

Economic analysis indicates that implementation of the OFMP is expected to yield approximately NRs 48,000 per hectare per year, whilst the existing protection forest management provides an estimated return of only NRs 875 per hectare per year. Moreover, returns from the existing forest management are non-sustainable, as forest area and productivity decline over time. The analysis also projects that about 3000 person-years of jobs would be created annually as a result of the OFMP. However, the plan should also specify other benefits which accrue from implementing it.

Silvicultural Practices

The plan describes silviculture activities in detail and provides tabular summations of the work envisaged by time and costs. Silviculture activities should be described in more detail in silviculture guidelines. A summation of how these might affect the environment and how negative impacts will be overcome by changes in operational activities should be included in the plan. The interaction between silviculture activities and the protection and conservation of plant and animal habitats should be better determined and explained.

Summary of the Analysis

Table 8.5 summarises the values assigned to these impacts, and their significance. Many of the impacts predicted for both alternatives are easily recognised, but lack hard data for use in a more definitive analysis. Baseline data describing impacts under the current situation vary in quality; some are well developed and quantitative, such as the silviculture information and initial work on water quality in Halkhuriya Lake. Other aspects have never been quantified, for example impacts on wildlife populations and the impacts of grazing and burning. Such aspects can only be described qualitatively, based on the best available professional opinions. Consequently, it is difficult to make effective comparisons between the various impacts at any level.

For many issues, the positive impacts under the current situation appear to be less than the negative impacts. However, for the second alternative, many issues show more positive and fewer negative impacts. Summing the overall impact values in Table 8.5 indicates that, for the first alternative, the negative impacts outweigh the benefits by −1080, whereas for the second alternative positive impacts outweigh negative ones by +1047. However, these figures should be used with caution, since there may be bias in the way that workshop participants assigned values. Despite this, the general consensus of those involved was that these values give a good basic framework for analysis in the absence of numerical data (IUCN/Nepal, 1995).

Mitigation and Protection Measures

Most of the negative impacts associated with the first alternative are severe and difficult to overcome without significant changes in existing conditions. Implementation of the OFMP would bring significant changes, and would eliminate or reduce most of the adverse impacts associated with the first alternative; however, it is also likely to produce several adverse impacts which can be reduced by the careful planning and execution of activities.

For each impact associated with the second alternative, cost-effective measures to minimise adverse effects need to be designed and included in the OFMP. These mitigation measures should include:

- proposals to involve the local people affected;
- strategies to control burning, poaching, fuel wood gathering and grazing;
- an inventory of environmentally sensitive areas; and
- strategies for biodiversity conservation.

There are some issues associated with the first alternative which even the implementation of the second alternative would not eliminate, including wildlife poaching, fuel wood collection, forest encroachment and grazing. These issues may need to be addressed on a piecemeal basis by introducing a new set of activities.

Monitoring and Evaluation

The mitigation measures prescribed above should form an integral part of the final plans and operational activities. To ensure that what was planned actually happens with the magnitude, extent and duration predicted, it is important to monitor many different aspects of the plan's implementation. Monitoring should be used to examine whether the plan's goals and objectives are achieved, prescribed activities are being implemented, and results produced address the issues and impacts. This will yield quantitative data about what changes took place.

Following monitoring, these results should be evaluated and compared with what was initially desired or predicted. Evaluations should be carried out periodically to ensure that the intended management direction is still valid and is being fulfilled as planned. Typically, detailed evaluations should take place every five years so that plans can be amended as necessary to meet evolving goals.

Table 8.5 *Impact Values Assigned to the Nineteen Issues**

Issue	Alternative 1		Alternative 2		Significance
	positive	negative	positive	negative	
1. Involvement of people	45	140	100	25	H
2. Uncontrolled burning	35	100	100	25	H
3. Wood poaching	50	140	100	25	H
4. Wildlife poaching	25	140	100	100	H
5. Fuel wood collection	100	90	140	35	H
6. Clearing forest land	100	140	140	75	M
7. Employment	50	100	140	90	H
8. Transportation	50	90	60	25	M
9. Grazing	50	100	75	25	H
10. Health	–	100	100	60	M
11. Erosion	35	100	100	25	H
12. Biodiversity	–	100	100	100	H
13. Tenure	60	100	60	50	H
14. Legal and institutional matters	140	140	125	75	H
15. Harvesting methods	50	100	140	40	H
16. Economic activity	50	140	140	100	H
17. Awareness and education	90	140	140	50	H
18. Silviculture methods	90	140	140	90	H
19. Marketing strategies	140	140	140	75	H

* H = high; M = moderate

Preferred Alternatives and Recommendations

The current condition of Bara District forest is not acceptable socially, environmentally or economically. If the current situation continues, the forest will be degraded within 25 years (Parajuli, 1994). Two alternatives were assessed, and for each one negative and positive impacts were evaluated. The OFMP has considerable merits if it is successfully implemented; in particular, it would mitigate the negative impacts seen under current conditions. The negative impacts associated with the OFMP are likely to be easily mitigated provided that technical, financial and political supports are in place. Impacts which cannot be mitigated are less severe and of shorter duration than those occurring under the first alternative.

The SEA thus concludes that:

- the second alternative (the OFMP) should be implemented;
- the OFMP contains acceptable data to be used for silviculture and harvesting practices;
- the OFMP lacks several important costings. Those outlined in the current OFMP only cover timber management aspects. However, costs for training and education, biodiversity conservation, employing local people, transitional costs for tenure rights and social implications, and logistic supports should be included in a revised OFMP; and
- the OFMP lacks goals and objectives. It should be amended to include all important parameters related to forest management, develop more baseline data, recommend changes in policy and legislation, involve affected people, and develop silviculture and harvesting regimes.

In a nutshell, the current OFMP is a timber management plan rather than a forest management plan, and lacks consideration of biophysical, social and cultural aspects related to forest resource utilisation. To make it comprehensive, the aspects outlined above should be incorporated in the revised OFMP.

Acknowledgements

This study was partially supported by FINNIDA Nepal. The authors wish to express their gratitude to the government of Finland. The authors are also grateful to Dr Julian Dunster, EIA advisor, IUCN/Nepal, for his help in completing this study, and to Paddy Gresham, chief of EIA Service, and Dr Jeremy Carew Reid, head of Conservation Division, IUCN-HQ, Gland, Switzerland, for their generous moral and financial support. The authors also thank the consultants who were involved in the study and those who participated and contributed substantially in the workshop and field study for their contributions. Finally, we are grateful to the Department of Forestry and FMUDP, who gave us permission to publish this work.

Part III

SEAs of Comprehensive/Area-Based
Plans

9
SEA of Hertfordshire County Council's Structure Plan

John Rumble and Riki Thérivel

Introduction

This chapter discusses the SEA for Hertfordshire County Council's structure plan. Hertfordshire is a mixed urban and rural area, covering some 164,000 hectares. It is located to the north of London and has one of the highest population densities, outside of the major cities, in the UK. It also has the second highest level of car ownership of any of the shire counties.

A structure plan is one form of local authority development plan in the UK, the other types being district local plans or unitary development plans. These plans in turn are generally composed of broad strategies for the location of development, which are then interpreted as more specific policies. In structure plans, these policies focus on strategic issues, while local plan policies are more location-specific. SEA of development plans is somewhat easier than other forms of SEA, in that development plans in the UK go through a distinct life cycle, lasting broadly five to ten years, with clear stages at which a plan is published and an SEA can be carried out. This chapter first reviews the British government's guidance for SEA of development plans. It then reviews the 'best practice' experience of Hertfordshire County Council, which has incorporated the principle of sustainable development into its structure plan through the SEA process.

UK Government Guidance Regarding SEA

The requirement for local authorities to carry out SEAs – or 'environmental appraisals' – of their development plans originated in 1990 with the British government White Paper on the Environment, *This Common Inheritance* (DoE, 1990), which stressed the importance of ensuring that environmental considerations are fully incorporated into policy development. Commitments made in the White Paper resulted in the publication of *Policy Appraisal and the Environment* (DoE, 1991) in September 1991. This booklet, aimed at central government mid-level managers, aimed to show 'how environmental effects can be taken into account in environmental and other policies'. The methodology it suggested involves:

- summarising the policy issue;
- listing the objectives;
- identifying the constraints;
- specifying the options;
- identifying the costs and benefits;
- weighing up the costs and benefits;
- testing the sensitivity of the options;
- suggesting the preferred option;
- setting up any monitoring necessary; and
- evaluating the policy at a later stage.

Although in theory this is a robust and comprehensive methodology, it has been found to be difficult to implement fully in practice. This can be deduced from the relative sparsity of findings in the DoE's booklet *Environmental Appraisal in Government Departments* (DoE, 1994), which reviews the activities resulting from *Policy Appraisal and the Environment*.

The publication of Planning Policy Guidance Note 12, *Development Plans and Regional Guidance* (DoE, 1992) in February 1992 marked the beginning of EA of local authority development plans in the UK. PPG12 suggests that local authorities should consider the environmental implications of their development plans, and highlights the role of development plans in helping to achieve sustainable development. It refers local authorities to the appraisal approach given in *Policy Appraisal and the Environment*.

In response, some local authorities began to carry out SEAs, albeit using much simpler techniques than those advocated by the government. These early SEAs provided the basis for *Environmental Appraisal of Development Plans: A Good Practice Guide* (DoE, 1993). This guide proposes a three-step SEA process:

- characterise the environment: identify and assess the environmental stock which could be affected by the development plan. The guide suggests 15

environmental components divided into those that relate to global sustainability, natural resources and local environmental quality;
- scope the plan: ensure that the plan covers an appropriate range of environmental concerns by comparing its policies to the requirements of existing government advice and other relevant guidelines; and
- appraise the plan content: determine whether the plan's objectives and policies are internally consistent, and assess their likely environmental effects, possibly using a variety of matrices.

Since then, many local authorities have carried out, or begun to carry out, SEAs of their development plans. By late 1995, at least 200 SEAs were at various phases of development, with more than 110 of these completed. Many of these SEAs are relatively simple documents which limit themselves to the steps set out in the good practice guide. However, some local authorities, including Hertfordshire, have developed an appraisal process that goes considerably beyond the guide's methodology. The most comprehensive of these SEAs include the following steps (although not always in this order):

- establish sustainability objectives;
- establish plan objectives (possibly with a matrix showing how the plan objectives relate to the sustainability objectives);
- compare locational alternatives;
- describe the environment and establish environmental criteria and/or indicators;
- scope the plan;
- test the plan strategy and policies with relation to the environmental criteria; and
- include/add specific environmental policies.

EAs of development plans are unusual in that they are a product of 'methodology forcing': the Department of the Environment essentially set the requirement for environmental appraisal of development plans before clarifying the methodology to be used. This is in contrast to the British government's generally cautious approach towards other forms of SEA, and particularly a mandatory Europe-wide SEA system. Although local authorities may have liked to receive more guidance early on about how to carry out their environmental appraisals, the resulting process is clearly suited to, and 'owned' by, local authorities.

Background and Scoping

Hertfordshire County Council's planning department started to review the county structure plan in 1993. Rather than modifying the old structure plan, a decision was made to prepare a new plan from scratch, using sustainability as the key starting point. This process was based on the results of several previous studies as is shown in Table 9.1. In 1992, Hertfordshire published the first comprehensive review of the state of the county's environment, and which provided a wealth of background knowledge. These findings encouraged the county council's strategic planning team to look more closely at some issues that would not normally feature high on the agenda.

Then, in early 1993, the county council commissioned CAG Consultants with Land Use Consultants to produce an environmental strategy for the county. This eventually became the link between the state of the environment report and the structure plan. The development of the strategy provided new ideas on how to approach the structure plan, particularly on issues which in the past had been dealt with away from the area of strategic planning. This helped to form the backbone of the structure plan strategy, as well as influencing the eventual environmental appraisal. In particular it prompted planners to use sustainability criteria rather than environmental stock criteria.

These reports allowed sustainability issues, and SEA, to be built into the plan from the beginning. Uniquely, the same people in the county council were involved in both of these reports, and also went on to develop the structure plan. Figure 9.1 shows how the environmental appraisal is linked to the plan-making process.

Source: Hertfordshire County Council, 1994

Figure 9.1 *Role of Environmental Appraisal in Hertfordshire County Council's Plan-making Process*

The reports also provided the technical basis for a discussion document entitled *Future Directions for Hertfordshire*, which was the result of a creative process in which planners aimed to critically evaluate the sustainability approach and some of the principles underlying Local Agenda 21, and to take these forward in the plan. In the spirit of Local Agenda 21, and as a way of helping to ensure that

Table 9.1 *Steps in Hertfordshire's Environmental Appraisal*

| Stage of plan making | Environmental appraisal | | |
	Defining environmental stock	Scoping	Appraisal of plan objectives and policies
Setting strategic aims and objectives	1992 – Hertfordshire 'State of the Environment' Report and annual updates 1993 – 'Environmental Strategy for Hertfordshire' Report 1994 – Indicators of positive impact expressed as a set of sustainability aims in Consultation Document	Land-use strategy, objectives, policies 1–39 and action plans drafted in the Consultation Document in order to move towards achieving sustainability aims	
Consultation Document and changes prior to Deposit			Stage 1 of the appraisal
Deposit Draft			Stage 2 of policy appraisal
Modifications after Examination in Public			Stage 3 of policy appraisal, if required
Monitoring and review after adoption of the Plan	Sustainability Indicators Project Structure Plan Annual Monitoring Reports from 1996 onwards		

Source: Hertforshire County Council, 1994

the plan's objectives are achieved, the county planners tried to ensure that a wide range of interests was represented and consulted during the plan-making process. Thus, *Future Directions for Hertfordshire* was used as a basis for a series of discussions with local groups. This 'soundings exercise' aimed to get the community involved in deciding how to achieve sustainable development in Hertfordshire, and to see how people reacted to the new approach proposed for the future planning of Hertfordshire.

Based on this consultation, five strategy objectives were developed which the plan seeks to achieve:

* to enable activities and development to be carried out in the most sustainable way;
* to improve the overall quality of life;
* to encourage people to make sustainable choices;
* to allow the same degree of choice for the future; and
* to contain consumption of, and damage to, natural resources.

Almost everyone agreed with these objectives, although there was extensive debate about what they mean in practice, particularly about the term 'sustainability'. For the purposes of the plan, the Brundtland Commission's definition – ensuring that the needs of the present are met without compromising the ability of future generations to meet their needs (WCED, 1987) – was used rather than the concept of carrying capacity. However, the definition was further interpreted and expanded in the strategy at the beginning of the plan.

The Plan Vision, Aims and Objectives

A vision of Hertfordshire was then prepared, based on these five strategies. The following quotes give an indication of the tone of this vision:

> *During the [Soundings exercise]... many people felt that, despite an increase in our standard of living over the last thirty years, our quality of life had deteriorated. Hertfordshire is busier, dirtier, more dangerous, has fewer local facilities, and has less sense of community, they said. A principal aim of this review must be to ensure that similar complaints are not being made in thirty years' time... The vision of this Review is therefore of a Hertfordshire with distinct and diverse communities, each with their separate physical, social and cultural identity. Population and employment in each town would be balanced to allow people more chances of working close to where they live. Towns would also have a broad range of shopping, service and leisure facilities... In tomorrow's Hertfordshire the most common forms of transport for short distances would be walking and cycling.*

Much information on the condition of the county's natural and built environments had already been collected for the state-of-the-environment report. This, together with the Department of the Environment's (1993) advice, provided the basis for a set of environmental stock criteria by which Hertfordshire's environment can be characterised, as well as indicators of positive impacts on these stock criteria. Some of these are shown at Table 9.2. In addition to environmental criteria, quality of life issues – social, economic, cultural and spiritual –

Table 9.2 *Some of the Environmental Stock Criteria and Indicators of Positive Impact*

Global sustainability	
(primarily atmospheric and climatic stability and biodiversity issues)	

Transport energy efficiency – trips	1	Reducing trip length
	2	Reducing the number of motorised trips
Transport energy efficiency – modes	3	Increasing public transport share
	4	Increasing the attraction of walking and cycling
Wildlife habitats	11	Safeguarding designated sites (eg sites of special scientific interest and local nature reserves)
	12	Increasing general wildlife potential (eg corridors)

Local environmental quality
(conservation of local environmental quality concerned with the protection and enhancement/ retrieval of local environmental features and systems ranging from landscape and open space to cultural heritage)

Landscape and open land	21	Enhancing designated areas (eg areas of outstanding natural beauty)
	22	Enhancing general landscape quality
	23	Retaining countryside/open land
Urban environment 'liveability'	24	Enhancing townscape quality
	25	Increasing safety and sense of security
	26	Improving aural and olfactory environment

Source: Hertfordshire County Council, 1994

were considered. Thus the criteria used have been sustainability criteria rather than environmental criteria, and the appraisal is more a sustainability appraisal than an environmental appraisal. Based on the overall strategy for the county, a set of sustainability aims was developed (examples are shown across the top of Table 9.3). Each sustainability aim corresponds to indicators of positive impact, which are shown in brackets. For instance:

A reduce overall demand for resources, including land (1, 2, 19 and 30);
B make the most efficient use of non-renewable resources, including land (12, 21, 22, 24, 29 and 30);
O increase community awareness and involvement;
P improve equality of opportunity in economic and social terms.

The aims encompass all of the indicators of positive impact. However, the scope of the aims is wider than that particular set of indicators, particularly in

Table 9.3 *Part of Matrix Showing Relationship Between Plan Objectives and Sustainability Aims*

Structure plan objectives	Overall sustainability aims				
	A Reduce overall demand for resources (including land)	B Make the most efficient use of non-renewable resources (including land)	C Increase the use of renewable resources	D Increase the re-use and recycling of resources	E Maintain biological diversity
1 Make provision for homes needed now and in the plan period		✔			
2 Allow for wealth creation in the county while providing for the work needs of the population		✔			
3 Maintain the settlement patterns of small to medium-sized towns	✔	✔		✔	
4 Concentrate development in towns	✔	✔		✔	✔
5 Make towns pleasant and convenient places to live in, work in and use					

Source: Hertfordshire County Council, 1994

regard to aims regarding social impacts and equity (eg aims O and P). Directly and indirectly, the achievement of these more socially oriented aims can be expected to impact positively on the environment. For this reason, they are regarded as equally relevant to a sustainability appraisal.

By law, structure plans must be concerned primarily with strategic land-use matters. On the other hand, the sustainability objectives derived from Hertfordshire's vision addressed a much wider area of influence and dealt with sustainability in a much more comprehensive manner. For the purposes of the structure plan, the sustainability aims were expressed in the form of structure plan objectives which translate sustainability into land-use-related terms. Some of these are shown on the left side of Table 9.3. The entire table shows that each of the structure plan objectives helps to achieve one or more of the sustainability aims, and that all of the sustainability aims are addressed by one or more of the plan's objectives. Thus the sustainability objectives provided the framework for devising and refining policies and programmes for inclusion in the plan. However, the vision and the sustainability aims provide a picture of how the future could be, and are thus equally applicable to other areas of county council activity, as well as to the activities of other agencies.

Based on the plan objectives, specific draft policies were developed. Some of these are specifically environmental, for instance:

> *In order to preserve those assets whose loss or damage would produce significant and irreversible change for the worse, the following, including appropriate buffer zones around them, will be protected from development or proposals of any nature which could cause loss or permanent damage and will be managed to ensure their continuing value...*
>
> *The cumulative effect of development or other proposals on an area should maintain the balance of, or improve, the overall environmental stock of the area in terms of the natural and built environments, landscape and water resource and should recognise the mutual interdependencies of these various elements (Hertfordshire County Council, 1994).*

The vision, sustainability aims, structure plan objectives and draft plan policies were published in an informal consultation document of May 1994. They were then tested through another 'soundings' process carried out by consultants, who also commented on Hertfordshire's work to date. A leaflet on the subject was made widely available, and a six-month road show was taken around shopping centres. Slightly more than 1 per cent of Hertfordshire's population was contacted for a quality response (ie not just distributing the leaflet): this is quite amazing for a structure plan. This consultation resulted in some changes in emphasis, for instance giving more importance to jobs. Environmental groups were also contacted, and were largely very supportive.

The Formal Environmental Appraisal

In contrast to these early stages, which were primarily carried out by the planners who had prepared the consultation documents and written the draft policies, an attempt was made to get an independent view at a 'formal' EA stage. This SEA was thus carried out in-house by someone who was not originally associated with the plan, albeit in close consultation with the original planners.

The assessor first appraised the plan's development strategy. Three options had been put forward at the consultation stage: new settlements, peripheral expansion of towns and urban regeneration. Hertfordshire has approximately 30 small to medium-sized towns, the biggest of which has about 85,000 people, and more space had to be found for new houses. In part as a result of the SEA, the county decided to promote the option of urban regeneration.

For each of the plan's 39 policies, a policy appraisal was then carried out which considered (a) whether the policy would have any adverse effects on the achievement of the plan's sustainability aims, and (b) whether any adverse or problematic impacts resulted because of an incompatibility between policies. Table 9.4 shows part of the appraisal for one of the policies. The left column considers if the policy would have beneficial, uncertain or adverse effects on sustainability; for this, planners needed to think 30 to 50 years ahead. The right column considers whether the policy would be compatible with the implementation of each of the other 38 policies. A particular policy may itself have only beneficial direct effects on achieving sustainability aims, yet it might be incompatible with the successful implementation of another policy because of indirect and previously unforeseen secondary effects. The central column provides explanatory text relating to those effects which are considered to be adverse or uncertain, or where incompatibility between policies has been identified. This formal SEA stage only provided for a broad-brush assessment. It did not try to tie policies to specific impacts, but summarised the likely impact of the policy.

Overall, the 39 draft policies were found to be broadly beneficial in their effect on the plan's aims, and compatible with each other in terms of their environmental impacts. However, the appraisal did identify some policies with adverse impacts on sustainability, and/or incompatibility with other policies. Some issues raised by the appraisal were:

- Did the plan really address the issue of whether housing was needed, or did it merely follow the regional guidance to fulfil the demand for more housing? This raised issues of how lower-tier plans and SEAs can be carried out effectively in the absence of higher-tier SEAs; in this case, no SEA had been carried out for the national household projections, which essentially had to be taken as being equivalent to requirements for housing supply.
- Road development will always cause adverse environmental impacts, but

the plan had to include policies for such development.

- Hertfordshire is made up of about 60 per cent green belt. This division between built-up areas is a problem because it contributes to degradation due to lack of use, and to problems around urban fringe areas. However, the public is strongly in favour of green belts, so green belt policies cannot be removed from the plan.

- The plan identified seven key sites for economic – primarily commercial/industrial – development. This was seen as the major selling point for the county. However, these policies' benefits were mainly employment related, and they were shown to be a problem environmentally. The county is now looking at more mixed uses for these sites, and is trying to ensure that the issue of accessibility to these sites is addressed at an early stage.

- Hertfordshire has a major mineral resource, with which it has to make a national contribution: this affects non-renewable resources and leads to environmental impacts. Once minerals are extracted, there is also an opportunity for waste disposal. However, 75 per cent of the county sits atop of a major aquifer, so this can also cause problems.

The results of this SEA were published in December 1994. The next SEA stage will involve an SEA of the deposit draft plan, since as a result of the consultation draft's SEA and public consultation, the new plan is likely to be significantly different from the old one. This SEA will highlight the impacts of the proposals for change that result from the deposit stage of consultation. Its results will then feed into the next stage of plan-making.

Issues in Environmental Appraisal

Hertfordshire County Council has taken a radical approach towards sustainability. Its application of the principles of sustainability to the land-use planning process, in the form of the new structure plan for Hertfordshire, are innovative and revolutionary. The true test of these principles will be how they are finally implemented, and this must be through the medium of local plans and the development control process. It still requires much persuading to get the professionals in these areas to set aside their traditional quantitative and scientific approaches, and adopt a more qualitative view of the future of planning. It would not be appropriate to expect everyone to come on board straight away, and many both within the planning profession as well as outside it, need to be convinced. There are still several hurdles to be overcome within Hertfordshire. The plan must stand the test of an examination in public, where its guiding principles will be put under close scrutiny by planners and developers alike.

Hertfordshire's experience with SEA has raised some issues regarding the

Table 9.4 *Example of Compatibility of Plan Policies and Environmental Criteria*

Policy 10: Reduction in growth of car usage
The local authorities will aim to reduce the growth in car usage, especially during peak periods and in towns, through policies in this plan aimed at reducing the need to travel and encouraging the use of less damaging forms of transport, the County Council's Transport Policies and Programmes (TPP) and other programmes.

Achievement of sustainability aims	Commentary*	Compatibility with other policies
Key O No significant effect ✓ Beneficial effect ✓? Likely beneficial effect ✗ Adverse effect ? Uncertainty of prediction or knowledge ✓ A Reduce overall demand for resources ✓ B Make the most efficient use of non-renewable resources O C Increase the use of renewable resources O D Increase the re-use and recycling of resources O E Maintain biological diversity ✓ F Apply aims A–D in relation to energy efficiency ✓ G Mitigate the possible effects of greenhouse gases O H Increase the rate of carbon fixing	**Policy 4** See commentary on Policy 4. Some of the 20 'main' settlements listed in that policy are relatively small. Concentrating most new development in only the larger and so generally more transport-efficient settlements may be more compatible with Policy 10 than allowing substantial new development in all 20 settlements. **Policies 5, 6 and 7** See combined commentary on policies 5, 6 and 7. Much depends on the strategy which is chosen. Peripheral growth would probably be least effective in seeking to reduce the growth in car usage. Exceptions to this could be locations which can be shown to be particularly transport-energy efficient, such as close to major passenger transport infrastructure – or potentially so with new infrastructure provision. **Policy 33** See commentary on Policy 33. The choice of four of the six	**Key** ✓ Compatibility ✗ Incompatibility ? Uncertainty ✓ 1 Whole settlement strategies ✓ 2 Town centres ✓ 3 Green belt ? 4 Development: main settlements ? 5 & 6 Development strategy ? 7 Distribution of new dwellings ✓ 8 Affordable housing ✓ 9 Design and form of new development ✓ 11 Primary routes: traffic and improvements ✓ 12 Improvements to other roads ✓ 13 Construction of new roads ✓ 14 Pedestrian, bus and cycle networks ✓ 15 Environmental areas (for transport planning) ✓ 16 Public transport ✓ 17 Assessment of development: transport impacts ✓ 18 Car parking provision

- ✓ I Reduce the effects of pollution
- O J Maintain the capacity of land to renew itself
- O K Maintain critical national and local assets
- O L Maintain stocks of less critical assets
- ✓ M Improve the overall quality of life
- O N Ensure that needs for shelter and economic support are met
- ✓? O Increase community awareness and involvement
- ✓ P Improve equality of opportunity

'key' employment sites is incompatible with development site selection on the basis of seeking to reduce the growth in car usage and encourage the use of other, less damaging forms of transport.

Appraisal summary

Policy 10 is particularly important. However, it is incompatible with Policies 33 and 38, and could also conflict with Policies 4, 5, 6 and 7, depending on the development strategy which is chosen.

- ✓✓ 19 Rail and water freight depots
- ✓✓ 20 Protection of critical environmental assets
- ✓✓ 21 Chilterns Area of Outstanding Natural Beauty
- ✓✓ 22 Cumulative impacts on environmental outlook
- ✓✓ 23 Landscape regions
- ✓✓ 24 Mineral deposits: non-sterilisation of reserves
- ✓✓ 25 Restoration of damaged land
- ✓✓ 26 Open spaces in towns: protection and provision
- ✓✓ 27 Tree cover
- ✓✓ 28 Water: catchment management plans
- ✓✓ 29 Renewable energy: provision of facilities
- ✓ 30 Aggregates: secondary and primary sources
- ✓✓ 31 Waste
- ✗ 32 Employment: development proposals
- ✓ 33 Employment: key sites
- ✓✓ 34 Retail development
- ✓✓ 35 Sports and recreation development
- ✓✓ 36 Rights-of-way network
- ✓✓ 37 Regional parks
- ✗ 38 Trunk roads programme: major investment
- ✗ 39 Other roads: county transport schemes

Source: Hertfordshire County Council, 1994

* Only some examples are shown here.

appraisal process:

- Should one carry out an environmental appraisal or a sustainability appraisal? Hertfordshire opted for sustainability appraisal because economic, social and cultural issues cannot be divorced from environmental issues: for instance, the need for new houses has an impact on mineral extraction, land use and pollution.
- Most of the SEA's conclusions were fairly obvious, and could have been reached without doing an appraisal. The SEA is also a relatively superficial and qualitative analysis, which is not so much an environmental analysis as an indicator of likely future change.
- Most of the appraisal's recommendations cannot be dealt with by a structure plan. In some cases they require implementation at the local plan level, and work is being instigated jointly with district councils to determine how the development strategy might be implemented. For instance, the county council is carrying out pilot work on 'whole settlement strategies' to broaden out the role of the planning process. Other issues, such as housing allocations or road construction, are determined at the national government level. Still others require cooperation with groups such as the Environment Agency. To implement the vision it must be applicable to a wide range of strategies and programmes and must be seen as a guide to all of them. Ownership amongst a wide group of stakeholders is key to successful implementation.
- Hertfordshire County Council's Structure Plan Policy Panel has a long tradition of wanting to do something new and state-of-the-art, and was very supportive of the SEA process. A panel of about ten members met once a month, and was kept informed all along. Had this not been the case, the plan would not have gained support.
- Project EIA has not been specifically linked to the plan SEA. This link was felt to be suspect, because EIA and plan appraisal are very different tools: one deals with generalities and overall impacts, whilst the other deals with specific issues in a mostly quantitative manner.

SEA is a useful tool for plan development and must be seen as an integral part of the process. It provides a mechanism to evaluate the plan's impacts, to adjust accordingly where the likely outcomes do not meet the plan's overall objectives and to guide any mitigation measures necessary. It should also clarify where policies that do not 'fit' into the plan originate (eg Department of Transport roads policies). If it is done as an add-on process with no feedback into the plan, then it is merely a wasteful exercise carried out to comply with regulatory requirements.

The major advantage of Hertfordshire's SEA was that it provided the planning team with some good ideas, suggested some answers, raised a lot of questions and involved the public. It identified many issues that are not usually included in a standard structure plan. Rather than dealing with 'traditional' specific policies (eg on employment or housing), the new policies focus on sustainable development, whole settlement strategies, and issues about quality of life and assets. As such, the SEA has truly helped to incorporate the principle of sustainability into Hertfordshire's structure plan.

10
SEA: Integration with Municipal Comprehensive Land-use Planning in Sweden

Eva Asplund and Tuija Hilding-Rydevik

Introduction

The local political unit in Sweden is the municipality, of which there are about 280. Compared with corresponding political levels in many other countries, Swedish municipalities hold an important position in community planning. This is related in part to their right of taxation, and in part to their sole right to plan where, when and how urban settlements may be established. According to the Swedish Planning and Building Act (PBA) and Natural Resources Act (NRA), municipalities are responsible for the maintenance and improvement of the quality of the built and natural environment. The PBA also requires all municipalities to provide a comprehensive land-use plan (CP) that covers the entire municipality, although certain parts of the plan may be analysed in more detail.

It is at this comprehensive level of planning that significant choices are made for the future development of the municipality. This is also the level at which decisions are made concerning how, for instance, national environmental goals should be implemented. Decisions for the future use of land, water and other natural resources must be taken, and optional strategies politically tested. The CP should therefore be used as an instrument to consider the impacts of alternative policies, since the opportunities to discuss alternative ways of achieving goals and finding different solutions is still relatively good. Both long- and short-term considerations should be taken into account. These are the reasons why an integration of SEA in comprehensive planning is especially interesting.

This chapter presents the results of a research project based on two case studies conducted mainly during 1992 and 1993. The research was based on international experience with project EIA and a wish to gain practical experience of testing EIA concepts as a way of reforming the comprehensive land-use planning process. The following ideas underpinned the study:

- SEA must be integrated in the comprehensive land-use planning process.
- SEA must start very early in the planning process.
- Alternative plans must be considered and presented to the decision-makers.
- The study methodology – for instance choices concerning scoping and rejected alternatives – must be made clear in the SEA document.
- Early scoping must be carried out with help from the public.
- The SEA document must be reviewed by some independent party.
- The SEA process should be based on qualified and structured dialogues instead of sophisticated methods for prediction and assessment.

The main purpose was to find out whether SEA could be integrated into the planning process, and how it would affect the process, the different professionals and the final decisions.

The Action

The case studies involved SEA of the CPs for special parts of two municipalities, Sollentuna and Karlskoga. In Sollentuna the planning commission was to provide outlines for an appropriate policy for future land use in Margareteborg, an almost unexploited part of the community (some 200 hectares), located on the waterside. The task was to make proposals for the location of housing, employment sites, transport infrastructure etc., and to consider the amount of housing needed (Municipality of Sollentuna, 1993).

In the case of Karlskoga, the municipality was planning for a new railway for fast regional and long-distance trains (between Stockholm and Oslo, the capitals of Sweden and Norway). The commission was to plan the location of the railway line and a new station in the town of Karlskoga. From the start, all the political parties were convinced that the railway project was urgently required in order to guarantee the consolidation of the municipality through improved accessibility to the regional labour market and educational facilities (Larsson et al, 1993).

We started collaborating with the two municipalities in order to gain experience of using SEA as a specific tool in comprehensive land-use planning in practice. Our participation and observations were brought to an end at the moment the political decision had been taken. The results and conclusions presented here are the synthesis of our experiences from both of the case studies. The SEA process, and our intervention in the planning process, were recorded through notes from meetings, a working diary and tape recordings. Finally, interviews (by a researcher not involved in the case studies) were used to record and analyse the effects in practice.

SEA and Planning Legislation in Sweden

Although there are no regulations requiring an SEA of the comprehensive land-use planning process in Sweden, voluntary SEAs of CPs have been carried out since the early 1990s in several municipalities. The PBA is presently being revised, and will probably place a legal demand for impact assessment on all CPs. To date, the Swedish regulations on SEA for actions other than projects concern national investment plans for infrastructure (roads and railways), detailed development plans (where the competent authority is the municipality), municipal energy supply plans, methods used in forestry and fishery, and rules for national authorities. The two case studies were based on the existing regulations (PBA and NRA) and practice in the comprehensive land-use planning process (see Figure 10.1).

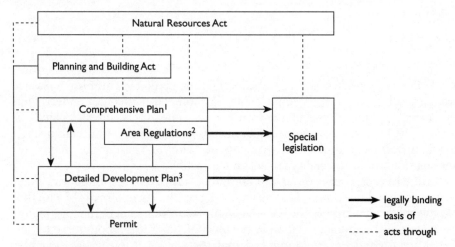

1 The comprehensive plan is the basis for assessing permit applications in accordance with the Planning and Building Act (PBA), and assessing other issues in accordance with the Natural Resources Act (NRA).
2 Area regulations within specified areas of the comprehensive plan.
3 The comprehensive plan can also give guidance in the drafting of a detailed development plan, but the content of the DDP does not need to agree with the comprehensive plan.

Source: Engström, 1991

Figure 10.1 *The System of Plans for Physical Planning in Sweden*

To the existing planning procedures we also added EIA/SEA requirements such as an early start, consideration of alternatives (including the 'no-action' alternative), early public participation and an independent review of the SEA document. To overcome prejudice concerning the importance of environmental issues, we used dialogues as a means of feed-back between environmental experts (municipal officials and our own experts), urban planners, economists, engineers etc.

The concept of sustainable development was used as the basis by which environmental impacts were analysed. Generally, attempts to define the concept are futile: we wanted to test whether an understanding of sustainable development could be more easily obtained by dialogues based on specific cases. The application of the concept as a pedagogic tool in the dialogue and in the scoping of key issues should also be evaluated.

The Domain of SEA or Who is the Decision-Maker?

The case studies showed that the officials in the planning process have a crucial influence on plan results, mainly through the alternatives they put forward to the politicians. The drafting of the plan proposals, together with impact assessment, is a process in which many different alternatives worth considering are identified. Formally, the final decisions are to be taken by the politicians. However, in practice, significant decisions are concealed from the formal decision-makers through, for example, the scoping of alternatives to be considered. This situation occurs because Swedish planning legislation regulates the procedure (formal authorisation of the plan) and not the process of plan-making (no qualitative claims concerning the planning process and the plan). Furthermore, political goals and intentions for planning activities are generally vague or absent. The problem of formulating goals and/or making general goals operational is normally handed over to officials. This problem of delineating the decision domain between officials and elected politicians is probably a general problem which also affects other planning processes and levels. Integration of SEA in existing planning processes also makes this a problem for SEA.

In our case studies, we were able to study how the process of plan drafting was affected by, and how municipal officials reacted to, the integration of SEA in the plan-making process (Figure 10.2). The case studies show how the reactions of the officials affected the information communicated to politicians and the public. In the interviews, we also recorded the reaction of the politicians to the content of the SEA report.

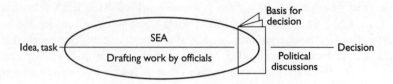

Note: The initiative for a CP for a restrictive part of the municipality can come from officials, elected politicians or the public. The domain of implementing SEA in the comprehensive planning process is in the drafting of plan proposals by officials.

Figure 10.2 *Simplified Scheme of the Comprehensive Planning Process*

Early Integration is the Key to the Full Potential of SEA

Early and Simultaneous Start of Plan Drafting and Impact Assessment

In the case-studies the practical implication of integration was understood as being continuous feedback between impact analysis and drafting of the plans, from the first informal meetings between the integrated planning and SEA team, through to the production of the SEA report and the plan proposal. Often EIA and SEA are seen merely as a way of assessing alternatives that have been derived from a planning process which is separate from EIA/SEA. Through integration we wanted to open up the early stages and the choices/decisions made there to the scrutiny of impact assessment. Only then it is possible to consider the full range of potential mitigation measures and to inspire the search for alternative solutions in the planning process. We designed the feedback to occur through personal communication – dialogues – rather than the more common procedures of sending documents out for consultation and receiving written feedback.

The case studies revealed that the integration of SEA in the comprehensive land-use planning process was totally dependent on how the very early stages in the planning process were carried out: who was present, at which occasions and with what authority. In our case studies the integrated planning and SEA team consisted of the municipal officials (urban planners who led the planning process, environmental experts, economists and engineers), consultants, we two researchers and our own environmental experts (EEG). We concluded that the following prerequisites are especially important for the integration of SEA in the comprehensive land-use planning process.

The influence on the results of the planning process is decided by participation and legitimacy. Those who participate in the early phases, when the key problems are identified and the search for alternatives starts, are the ones who actually decide the scope of the work to come – provided that everyone is given the legitimacy to contribute to the process. People involved later in the process do not have the same opportunity. Explicit and implicit choices made early in the process, and the growth of psychological barriers, diminish the possibilities to affect the process in the later stages.

For instance, in Sollentuna, an early 'brainstorming' meeting was arranged. Of the people taking part in these discussions, only the two leading municipal planners and the two consultants were later on the integrated SEA-CP working team. Key issues – including environmental issues – were picked out and discussed with no involvement of environmental professionals. The task of outlining two different alternatives was then entrusted to the consultants. The drafts were presented at the first meeting of the working team. One team member put the stress on biotechnical solutions (eg for water supply), while another promoted a more human ecological concept. A list of criteria put forward by the EEG had only a moderate influence on the search for alternative designs, since the consultants were already focused on defending their own proposals.

The plan drafting and the work of environmental experts must begin simultaneously. If not, the planning officials will be looked upon as the only ones who have the legitimacy to scope the plan. A simultaneous start also means having a broad representation of sectors and experts at the early decisive stages. The broad and integrated planning and SEA team must first decide actively and consciously which issues should be integrated and affect the drafting and SEA work. If this is not done, certain questions will not be considered. Also, formulating goals and intentions with the planning commission must be seen as an important and active process, since the goals will also delineate/scope the search for alternatives.

Alternatives Are the Keys to Relevance for Decision-Makers

Considering alternatives in drafting the plan allows new ways of avoiding or mitigating environmental impacts at a more strategic level to be discovered. In Karlskoga the search for alternatives throughout the process was based on analyses of environmental impacts. This dialogue led to a deeper understanding of what really were serious threats to sustainability and which impacts were temporary or possible to mitigate. Risks caused by mixing public and hazardous transport greatly affected the alternatives considered (six in all: five different routes, some including tunnels, plus the 'no-action' alternative.

In Sollentuna the most apparent effect of the dialogues was the identification of a political choice that had to be made: whether to construct a new railway station or not. Direct rail access to regional centres might not prevent car traffic, but it could make the new 'suburb' more sustainable (no need to own a car). A third alternative was outlined in order to clarify the pros and cons of connecting the new suburbs to the station, compared with previous drafts which proposed a local system of public transport with connections to existing railway stations. Data directly affecting the location of settlements, for instance baseline information on biologic diversity, were easier to handle than more complex information. Problems of pollution in Sollentuna from car traffic were clarified, but opinions about mitigation measures varied.

The discussions often became very emotional. One reason for this may have been a lack of skill in analysing social aspects of environmental impacts: SEA requires an analysis to be made of the complete impact chain of person-society-environment, in order to find alternatives that elucidate strategic choices. Another reason is that future policy for restricting car traffic is, in fact, a political question. The role of SEA should be to present feasible and policy-oriented alternative solutions, but the final decisions should be made by politicians.

The importance of 'no-action' alternatives as references is as important in SEA as in project EIA, but these alternatives can be harder to define, and more numerous, (see Table 10.1). We defined our 'no-action' alternative as the probable development if the proposed plan or action was not implemented (for instance keeping an area for recreational purposes). The assessment of the 'no-action' alternative may require an analysis of developments or actions resulting from decisions already made, during the time span of the proposed action. A comparison with a status quo situation is not of much value as a reference.

Analysis of Impacts and Comparing Alternatives

Identifying, scoping and actually analysing impacts was done by the environmental experts (municipal officials and the EEG) and us, in co-operation with the rest of the integrated planning and SEA team. The results from the continuous impact analyses were fed into the drafting of the plan and the search for new alternatives and mitigating measures.

In the case of Sollentuna the EEG identified seven criteria to be fulfilled in the plan in order to obtain sustainable development in the area in question. The criteria were based on good baseline information, political goals (eg protection of biological diversity) and thresholds of concern (eg acidification and noise). The alternative plan proposals were assessed according to these criteria by the EEG and environmental officials. The traditional way of presenting land-use plan proposals in maps did not offer a sufficient basis for the analysis. Possible effects of policy implementation, the sequence of development, economic and other regulations, mitigating measures etc also had to be addressed. Unfortunately, we were never able to complete the second stage of this analysis in Sollentuna.

In the case of Karlskoga the EEG did not define distinct sustainability criteria, mainly because sustainability was not just a matter of locating the railway but concerned the future of the whole municipality. This task was too demand-

Table 10.1 *Summing Up the Local Impacts of Alternative Proposals for Development in Margareteborg**

Alternatives	Criteria for sustainable development in Margareteborg						
	Limitation of effects on biological diversity	Limitation of emissions from traffic	Regard to special recreational values	Local management of water supply and sewage	Regard to valuable historical sites	Limitation of noise	Economising with energy, local supply possibility
	5	5	3	3	2	2	2
o No action alternative[h]	++[a]	++[b]	++[c]	++[d]	++[e]	+[f]	++[g]
I New station development	+	?	+	?	?	?	?
2 Recycling development	+	?	+	+	?	?	+
3 Seaside development	−	?	+	?	?	?	?

* The relative importance of the different assessment criteria is described by the score below it. Scores go from 1 to 5, with 5 meaning that the criterion is of utmost importance if sustainable development is to be obtained. The scoring in the table uses a scale with four degrees, describing the degree of acordance with the respective criterion: ++, totally consistent with sustainable development (SD); +, consistent with SD; −, unfavourable to SD

a Assuming that the further management of the area promotes biological diversity.

b Assuming that the charge from surrounding areas does not increase.

c Assuming that the area will still be accessible and attractive.

d The criterion aims at recycling of water. This will be maintained if the area remains unexploited.

e Assuming that these values are taken care of.

f Assuming that the noise from the surroundings does not increase.

g Economising with energy means: recycling, reduction of emissions from fossil fuels, reduction of transport etc. This criterion will not be affected if the area remains unexploited.

h In Sollentuna the 'no-action' alternative (no further exploitation of the area) could itself be divided into three possibilities: a total ban on development, development in other unexploited areas in the municipality or region, or a concentration on existing built-up areas in the municipality. Only the first 'no-action' alternative was used as a reference because the other alternatives were not interesting to the politicians at the time.

ing to fit into the research project. It was also more difficult because the environmental problems were not as evident and of the same scale as in the case of Sollentuna. The impact analysis thus involved more traditional project EIA questions such as the immediate impacts from construction and management.

In both cases the analysis was based on good baseline information, good local knowledge and best available professional judgement. In Karlskoga, matrices were used as working instruments by the integrated planning and SEA team to identify which criteria/standards/goals the railway needed to fulfil concerning function, economy and environment. The team used these criteria to assess the different alternatives. This work gave an improved understanding of the pros and cons of the different alternatives and of the impacts of the railway.

The Draft Plans and SEA Reports Reflect the Process

The draft plans and SEA reports reflect how the planning and SEA processes were integrated: political goals (where they existed), choices made by the officials and the research project concerning interpretation of goals, scoping of the draft plan and SEA work, choice of experts, and at what moments the experts and politicians were brought in and taken out of the process.

In the case of Sollentuna, we did not succeed in fully integrating SEA and the comprehensive land-use planning process. This was the first of the two case studies, and we were not prepared for the rapidity with which barriers (the 'don't kill my darlings' syndrome) could be erected. Neither were we aware of the importance of a simultaneous start. Accordingly. the SEA report (about 40 pages, prepared by us and one municipal environmental expert/official) became a supplement to the draft plans (about 20 pages). The connection between the draft plan and the SEA results was thus very weak.

In the case of Karlskoga, we were more prepared and the integration was successful. The process was manifested in one integrated report (about 55 pages, of which about 30 were supplements, prepared by the whole integrated planning and SEA team) in which the connections and feedback between draft plans and SEA results were clear. The integrated report was a better basis for decision for the politicians, because the process had led to the identification of the most significant questions, and questions of relevance for the politicians.

However, even in the case of Sollentuna, through the broad dissemination of the results of the draft plans and the SEA report (to other municipal committees, neighbouring municipalities, the county board, NGOs etc), the SEA report was generally seen as a very valuable input. For many readers, the length of the report was no problem. Politicians, on the other hand, would have preferred a more concise presentation.

The Results of the Integrated SEA and Comprehensive Land-Use Planning Process

In the case studies, the municipal officials became part of an integrated process. This process has helped to identify new and sometimes otherwise unforeseeable possible designs for the plan proposals. It has enabled the officials to produce an extended basis for decisions directed towards the politicians. It was thus possible to change the traditional way of planning (normally leading to one ultimate proposal) and of presenting plans (which stresses technicalities). The strategic import of planning activities has become obvious, and it has opened up the political debate on environmental values.

The municipal council is the supreme decision-making body in the municipalities. It works through the executive committee, which in our case studies functioned as both plan proponent and competent authority. The politicians on the executive committee participated in the process to a much lesser extent than did the municipal officials. They gave the officials an assignment, whose most concrete result was the draft plans and the SEA reports. It seems that the basis for decision was improved and appreciated as useful by the politicians when:

- strategic choices of great political concern were identified and reflected in alternatives presented to the decision-makers;
- a set of feasible alternatives was professionally assessed, compared and submitted as a basis for decisions;
- policies other than those considered in the plan proposals but of great significance for sustainable development were made clear; and
- SEA findings were integrated in the final plan proposal and presented in a clear, concise manner.

Creating Change Through Dialogue

Integrating SEA in the municipal comprehensive land-use planning process involves a reformation of the whole planning process. It requires, for example, that the role of different professionals be changed and that new kinds of materials be prepared as the basis for decisions. These changes may alter the existing balance of power between the officials concerned, as well as between the decision-makers.

In order to overcome these barriers, we used dialogues – face-to-face communication – as the means of feeding back throughout the process. In the two case studies, this dialogue helped to break down sectoral and professional departmentalisation, and raise the status of environmental issues. The SEA work revealed that the mitigation of environmental impacts was an interesting and useful task, and not just a hindrance to the planning process. Dialogue can replace much investigation at the comprehensive level, and we did not find any major need to quantify in our cases.

But it may take time to create a functioning dialogue. Successful integration – changing 'business as usual' – requires a sensitive handling of barriers to change among officials, professionals and politicians.

The barriers to integration lie mostly at the level of officials, and are to a certain degree built into the organisation. Politicians generally have an unclear picture of how the planning process is carried out. Officials are generally unaware of the connection between the planning process and how decisions are made. The difficulty of having a dialogue between professionals from different disciplines, with differing views of the relation between people and nature, is well known, but it is not accepted and therefore not dealt with in the planning process.

In the case studies, our deliberate role turned out to be that of coordinators and facilitators for the dialogue. It is likely that, in a transitional phase towards integration, external professional skills will be needed to facilitate and coordinate such dialogue. Once this experience is gained, the function can be taken over by the municipality; it must, however, be independent of the sectoral interests in the process.

Conclusions

The two case studies discussed here have shown that the integration of SEA in the comprehensive planning process can contribute to a general improvement and transformation of both the process and the results. Where the land-use planning process is well developed, reformation through the integration of SEA is more likely to lead to better solutions than through the creation of a separate SEA procedure. The experience of project EIA and separate procedures also points in this direction.

The integration of SEA in existing planning procedures makes its success dependent on, for example, the status of the system it is integrated to. In our cases the possibility for SEA to contribute to sustainable development was dependent on the CP's power to direct the use of land, water and air in the municipalities. It also depended on how well the planning process was tiered to the process of detailed development plans.

Any transitional phase towards integration means finding ways to change attitudes, overcome barriers and prejudices, and change the composition of professionals involved in plan-making. It is important to separate advice and recommendations for accommodating and achieving change from more formal rules and requirements for SEA. Trial runs and case studies with SEA in the municipal planning process should lead to the development of new routines and competences adapted to the needs of different municipalities. Legal demands for SEA are not enough to create a satisfactory SEA practice and implementation in the Swedish municipalities.

11
SEA of the San Joaquin County General Plan 2010, California, US

Amy Skewes-Cox

Introduction

This case study addresses the environmental impact report (EIR) on the general plan for San Joaquin County, a 1400-square-mile (3600 km^2) area located in California's great central valley. The general plan will guide land-use decisions extending to the year 2010. Unlike EIRs prepared for specific development projects, a 'planning programme' EA addresses general and cumulative impacts over a long time period, and can recommend mitigation measures that are more far-reaching than those for a specific project.

The General Plan

California's state laws require every county and city in the state to amend their general plan every five years. These general plans are required to identify the types and locations of specific land uses, including densities, to accommodate projected growth in residential and non-residential uses over a specific time frame. The San Joaquin County general plan had the following objectives:

- to conform with state planning law (Government Codes 65302–65303);
- to describe a vision of the future for the county and identify objectives and policies that will guide development and make that development consistent with the vision;

- to present population and employment projections for the year 2010 and identify appropriate locations and types of development that should occur to accommodate this projected growth; and
- to present a comprehensive, unified programme for development.

The general plan was prepared over a five-year period by both private consulting companies and staff of the county planning department. Between 1987 and 1990, the general plan was developed, and over 100 meetings were held with the public and elected officials. The draft general plan projected an increase in county population of over 383,000 persons (80 per cent of 1990 total) by the year 2010, as well as over 116,000 (64 per cent of 1990 total) new jobs from commercial and industrial development. Initially, the plan proposed to accommodate this growth within the seven existing cities. However, the county later decided to revise the plan to include five 'new towns' in the county that would accommodate 38,800 new housing units and provide an estimated 16,000 new jobs. It should be noted that the county's general plan, while addressing population and job growth in the incorporated cities within the county, cannot guide growth within the boundaries of those incorporated cities; each city has its own general plan.

In the case of the San Joaquin County general plan, the elected five-member Board of Supervisors was responsible both for certifying that the EIR met the requirements of the California Environmental Quality Act (CEQA) and for adopting the general plan itself. EIRs were prepared for two versions of the plan, and were taken into account in deciding on the final plan, which was approved in 1992.

California Environmental Quality Act

The CEQA of 1986 requires that local agencies, for all 'projects they intend to carry out or approve which may have a significant effect on the environment', must prepare an EIR and certify that it has met the requirements of the CEQA. The act defines 'projects' as including 'activities' undertaken by the agency; thus, an environmental impact analysis must be completed for discretionary actions such as approvals of new subdivisions, adoptions of new zoning ordinances and adoptions of general plans or general plan amendments.

The CEQA requires that an EIR must contain the following contents:

(a) The significant environmental effects of the proposed project.
(b) Any significant environmental effects which cannot be avoided if the project is implemented.
(c) Mitigation measures proposed to minimize the significant environmental effects...
(d) Alternatives to the proposed project.

(e) The relationship between local short-term uses of man's environment and the maintenance and enhancement of long-term productivity.
(f) Any significant irreversible environmental changes which would be involved in the proposed project...
(g) The growth-inducing impact of the proposed project'.
(State of California, 1986)

In particular, the CEQA requires that all 'significant' impacts be identified in the EIR, and that mitigation measures be recommended to reduce the impact to a less-than-significant level or to eliminate the impact altogether. Impacts that cannot be adequately mitigated must be identified in an EIR section entitled 'significant, unavoidable impacts'. If the EIR is certified and the project is allowed to go ahead with such significant unavoidable impacts, the decision-makers are required to make a 'statement of overriding consideration' for approval of the project. Such a statement may include findings that specific economic, social or other considerations make the mitigation measures or alternatives infeasible.

Selection Process for EIR Authors

The EIR is generally carried out by an organisation separate from that preparing the plan. For the San Joaquin County general plan, the county initially requested proposals from two or three consulting firms to complete an EIR on its first general plan. After a review of these proposals, the county selected Baseline Environmental Consulting located in Emeryville, California, to complete the first EIR at a total cost of about $70,000. The funding for this first EIR was totally from the county's general fund. This first EIR was never certified, because the county decided to revise its general plan to include the five new towns and consequently to complete a new EIR.

For the second EIR (San Joaquin CCDD, 1992), Baseline Environmental Consulting was retained without having to undergo a competitive bidding process due to the firm's familiarity with the county at that point and the need to prevent further delays. However, Baseline did prepare a formal cost estimate for the EIR process and was awarded a contract valued at $525,000, with the developers of the new towns providing all of this cost. At the conclusion of the process, the county had expended over US$2 million for preparation of its general plan and the EIR. Of this total amount, about $623,000 was spent on the EIR process.

Impact Assessment as Related to Planning: 'Did the Cart Come Before the Horse?'

While some environmental information was gathered during preparation of the county's general plan, this information did not determine carrying capacity for the county, nor did it result in maps of 'opportunities and constraints'. Instead, population projections and developers' proposals for new towns appeared to guide the development of the general plan.

Population projections were provided by the California Department of Finance, an agency that relies on past trends in population growth and an economic and demographic model to estimate population. Developers' proposals for five new towns were made independently of county staff, thus placing the staff in more of a 'reactive' than a 'proactive' planning position when these new towns were included in the general plan by the county Board of Supervisors.

While a carrying capacity analysis is an effective and rational planning tool to guide future development, one must review the local situation to ensure that this is appropriate. In the case of San Joaquin County, few natural constraints to development exist. A majority of the county is level land used for agriculture. Thus 'constraints' such as steep slopes, riparian corridors and forested areas are very limited. The more constraining elements for the county were found to be prime agricultural soils, poor air quality (largely exacerbated by urbanisation in adjoining upwind counties), a limited transportation network, poor groundwater quality, and limited surface water supplies and sewage treatment capacity. However, none of these constraints was used to contradict the population projections provided by the state Department of Finance. Instead, the county assumed that the projections were correct and then attempted to ensure that adequate land area was designated to accommodate this future population.

Major Impact Issues

Under CEQA, the following topics must be addressed:

- land use and planning;
- geology/soils/seismicity;
- hydrology and water quality;
- traffic/transportation;
- air quality;
- noise;
- cultural/archaeological resources;
- visual quality;
- public health and safety (hazardous waste, electromagnetic fields, etc);
- public utilities (water, wastewater, storm drainage);

- public services (fire and police protection, schools, libraries, hospitals);
- fiscal impacts (only as related to environmental impacts such as inadequate financing for wastewater treatment).

While all of these were addressed in the EIR for San Joaquin County, certain issues were found to be more significant than others due to local conditions. These critical areas, which are discussed below, included agricultural land impacts, traffic, air quality and biotic resources.

Prime Agricultural Land

Baseline information
San Joaquin County has some of the best agricultural soil in the US as well as a climate that allows production of a variety of crops. The quality of agricultural soils is identified and mapped by the State Department of Conservation, which showed that up to 47 per cent of the soils in the county (over 176,000 hectares) were considered 'prime agricultural soils', the highest ranking. Another 16 per cent (59,000 hectares) was considered 'unique' or 'of statewide importance'. Only 18.6 per cent was considered grazing land (also important in its own right), and 13 per cent was designated as 'urban', 'other lands, or 'water'.

Impact analysis
Thus, the first step undertaken by the EIR authors was to determine if more land than necessary had been identified for future projected growth. The authors did not question the projected population figures, but instead concentrated on identifying how much acreage would be needed to accommodate new residences and businesses. A number of assumptions were used regarding:

- number of single-family vs multifamily dwellings;
- average densities per residential unit;
- average densities of units per acre;
- average square footage for commercial and industrial operations; and
- average number of employees by types of jobs and by square footage of building area.

The analysis concluded that more than 15,100 hectares of prime farmland had been designated on the general plan map for future growth, which would provide enough land for more than 50,000 persons above the projected growth for the year 2010. Thus, impacts related to removal of prime agricultural land were determined to be 'significant'.

Mitigation measures
While removal of prime agricultural lands was determined to be a significant,

unavoidable impact if the project were approved, mitigation measures were recommended in the EIR to reduce the impact to some degree. The mitigation measures included:

- a requirement for an 'impact fee' for each acre of land developed, with fees to be used for purchase of development rights on agricultural land or to support agricultural land trusts. As an alternative, developers could be required to place agricultural lands in a trust to ensure protection for agricultural use;
- recommendations for new findings when a request is made to annex agricultural lands to an urban area regarding proximity to the urban area and consistency with projected growth;
- redesignating areas from residential/commercial designations to 'agriculture-urban reserve' until such lands are needed for development;
- increased minimum parcel sizes for agricultural zones to 32.4-hectare and 64.75-hectare parcels; and
- increased residential densities for county areas adjacent to cities, requiring coordination with land use planning under the jurisdiction of cities.

Traffic

Baseline information
Information regarding traffic 'levels of service' for major county roads was derived from traffic counts undertaken by the San Joaquin County Council of Governments. Levels of service were defined A through F, with A being free-flow conditions and F being low operating speeds and stoppages for long periods of time. Roadway segments with level-of-service deficiencies at peak travel hours were mapped as part of the EIR. In addition to descriptions of existing vehicular traffic conditions, the EIR included baseline data on bicycle routes, public bus service and passenger rail service.

Impact analysis
The standard of significance for traffic-related impacts focused on the potential for general plan growth to result in levels of service less than C on all county roads and D on freeways and state highways. To complete the impact analysis, a countywide travel demand model was updated and revised to develop projections of daily vehicle traffic volumes for the year 2010.

The conclusion of the analysis was that countywide vehicle trips would increase by 84 per cent between 1990 and 2010, which would adversely impact the ability of the transportation system to meet acceptable level-of-service standards and would increase the frequency of accidents. While planned road improvements were accounted for in the analysis and some assumptions were made regarding alternate transit to be used in the future, the conclusion was that major additional road improvements would be necessary to accommodate future traffic levels. Both financial and environmental constraints could limit the feasibility and extent of the needed improvements.

Mitigation measures
Mitigation measures for transportation-related impacts focused on:

• policies to reduce vehicular traffic and to promote transit-oriented development;
• requirements that specific plans for large developments address provisions for public transit service;
• development of a countywide trip reduction ordinance which would specify actions to reduce peak-period traffic generation at employment sites;
• growth control measures to limit the level and distribution of development and related road improvements;
• guidelines for new communities and other developments, to promote non-auto transportation;
• expansion of the public transit system within the county; and
• road widenings and other improvements as needed (assuming that the above mitigation measures are also implemented).

Air quality

Baseline information
Air quality in San Joaquin County has deteriorated over the years, largely due to increased traffic, both within and outside the county. Urbanisation of the counties adjacent to San Francisco (Alameda and Contra Costa counties) has led to increased traffic in counties upwind of San Joaquin County. Due to topographic and climatic conditions, the county has experienced high levels of ozone, carbon monoxide and PM-10 (suspended particulate matter), and California and US standards established for these pollutants were exceeded within the county. The EIR addressed existing air quality, using data provided by the local Air Pollution Control District. Some of this information was available from local monitoring stations placed throughout the county to monitor ozone, carbon monoxide, nitrogen dioxide, sulphur dioxide, PM-10 and lead.

Impact analysis
The standard of 'significance' established for air quality was based on whether the general plan's projected growth would contribute substantially to an existing or projected air quality violation. Violations of air quality standards were not used as significance criteria because the county already was exceeding existing standards. Thresholds of significance were also established by the local Air

Pollution Control District which identified specified pounds per day for carbon monoxide, ozone precursors and PM-10 emissions.

The conclusion of the analysis was that by 2010, growth projected by the general plan would have a significant impact on regional emissions of ozone precursors (reactive organic gases and oxides of nitrogen) and PM-10. In addition, the projected general plan growth was found to far exceed that projected by the regional attainment plans prepared by the Air Pollution Control District. These attainment plans had been prepared for ozone and carbon monoxide and PM-10, and identified how much reduction in emissions would be necessary to attain established standards. The attainment plans were based on population forecasts, vehicle miles travelled, economic activity and other factors influencing emissions.

Mitigation measures
As mitigation for identified air quality impacts, the EIR recommended:

• new policies for the general plan and an associated requirement for air quality mitigation plans for new developments producing more than 500 trips per day;
• new policies for cooperative agreements among adjoining counties, transportation agencies and regional planning agencies for the formation of a regional transportation system and encouragement of land use/employment patterns to minimise air pollutants; and
• development of growth management policies to meet the mandates of the California Clean Air Act and to phase (vs prevent) growth within the county.

Biotic Resources

Baseline information
Due to extensive agricultural operations, much of the native vegetative cover in San Joaquin County has been removed. However, a diverse assemblage of resident and migrant wildlife species and habitat types can still be found. The following five communities were identified and described for the county: (1) riparian community, (2) woodland community, (3) chaparral community, (4) grassland, and (5) wetlands, vernal pools and the Delta. Plant and animal species associated with each habitat type were summarised, and a map based on aerial photography was included in the EIR to show the general boundaries of the five habitat types.

Data regarding rare, threatened and endangered species (ie special-status species) were derived from the California Department of Fish and Game, a state agency which maintains the Natural Diversity Data Base (NDDB). The NDDB is an inventory of reported populations and sightings of special-status taxa and unique or sensitive natural communities such as vernal pools, riparian forest or freshwater marsh. Information for the NDDB is updated on a continual basis, and mapped on United States Geological Survey 7.5-minute quadrangles for the entire state of California. The EIR also included more detailed biological information for each of the five new towns, using data prepared by qualified biologists. These data were based on review of more detailed aerial photography (as compared with that used for assessing the entire county), augmented by field surveys.

Impact analysis
Potentially significant impacts related to biotic resources included: impacts on populations or critical habitats of special-status plant or animal taxa; substantial interference with the movement of any resident or migratory fish or wildlife species; and substantial reduction in habitat for fish, wildlife or plants. One of the most significant impacts identified was the conversion of about 15,000 hectares of existing habitat to urban habitat (refer to earlier discussion of agricultural impacts).

Mitigation measures
Some of the mitigation measures related to protection of biotic resources were:

• policies to promote the use of native trees and shrubs in landscaping, especially for county-maintained properties;
• policies to promote the protection of large habitat areas and connection (vs fragmentation) of habitat areas;
• regulations to protect wetlands, special-status taxa and 'heritage' trees;
• support of habitat restoration plans for special-status taxa and use of a database that identifies habitat types for such taxa (to cover areas that may not have had recorded sightings of special-status taxa); and
• land-use controls to delay development of new towns and to focus new development at the fringes of existing cities/communities.

Alternatives

The CEQA requires that alternatives to the proposed project be evaluated in the EIR. No specific number of alternatives is required, but they must be alternatives that would not result in more significant impacts than the proposed project (per an amendment to CEQA in 1993). For the EIR on the San Joaquin County general plan, the alternatives included 'no project' (which assumed no growth beyond what currently exists as well as another scenario of growth under the existing general plan), the 'city-centred growth alternative' (which did not include the five proposed new towns), and other alternatives which considered similar or reduced population/employment growth in specific regions of the county. For each of these alternatives, all topics were evaluated (ie land use, traffic, geology), and potential impacts were compared with those identified for the proposed project.

Results and Effectiveness of EIR

The EIR included numerous mitigation measures, some of which were implemented and others which were rejected by the county. Many of the recommended policy changes were made to the final draft of the general plan. However, many of the recommended regulations were not added to the county's Development Title prior to approval of the general plan. The Development Title contains zoning and other specific regulations related to land use and development. While these regulations may at some point be adopted, few of the recommended mitigation measures had been adopted within one year of the approval of the general plan.

Findings of Overriding Consideration

When a project is approved that entails significant, unavoidable environmental impacts, the decision-making body must present findings of overriding consideration. Many of the significant, unavoidable impacts associated with the general plan have been identified above, such as removal of prime agricultural land and significant traffic impacts. The county's findings of overriding consideration were brief, and focused on the following elements which were described as 'outweighing' the plan's significant, unavoidable environmental impacts:

- approval of the general plan was designed to accommodate the projected population growth as long as specific conditions were met by future developments such as provision of adequate water and sewer service, funding of necessary on-site improvements and reduction of environmental impacts to an acceptable level;
- approval of a Development Title (containing regulations) to protect the public's health, safety and welfare; and
- expansion of the industrial, commercial and housing opportunities for existing and future residents within San Joaquin County.

Perhaps one of the most effective uses of the entire EIR document has been as a resource for specific projects as they are proposed within the county. Instead of the document finding its way to a bookshelf and never being used again, the data have been helpful for a variety of subsequent projects.

Political Influence

In the end, the EIR did not sway the politicians to adopt the most environmentally sensitive general plan, which would have been the 'no-project alternative' or the 'city-centred growth alternative' (no new towns). With this latter alternative, the population would be 113,000 fewer persons and employment would be reduced by 16,500. Growth would occur within and at the fringes of cities. Instead, the general plan was approved with growth at the edge of existing communities plus two new towns which were probably the least 'environmentally-sensible' of the five new towns originally proposed. The exact reasons for this decision may never be known.

As of 1995, one the new towns which had been rejected initially obtained a general plan amendment, and was in the midst of obtaining final approvals prior to ground breaking. None of the other new towns had proceeded to the first stage of development of a specific plan, and growth within the county was almost at a standstill due to the general economic recession and slow rate of development throughout California. Staffing of the county planning department was significantly reduced due to budget shortfalls, leaving little if any progress with further implementation of the EIR's recommended mitigation measures.

Monitoring

A monitoring plan was incorporated into the EIR for all recommended mitigation measures. Table 11.1 shows an example of this. Some of the mitigation measures were able to be monitored simply at the time of adoption of the general plan (ie incorporation of recommended new or revised policies), while others needed to be monitored at the specific plan stage for the new towns, at the pre-construction stage such as tentative or final subdivision map approval, at the construction stage or finally at the operational stage of specific developments.

Conclusions

Environmental analysis at the planning stage, as compared with the specific development proposal stage, is critical for the following reasons:

- significant, cumulative impacts can be identified at an early stage and mitigation measures applied proportionally to future developments (ie specific mitigation fees based on size or intensity of development), as compared with piecemeal mitigation measures applied at the development stage;
- mitigation measures can focus on policy language as well as regulatory measures, thus providing an effective enforcement mechanism for mitigation measures;
- public awareness of major issues is increased, greatly aiding the political process; and

Table 11.1 *Examples of Mitigation Monitoring Programmes*

Impact	Mitigation measures	Monitoring requirements	Person/agency responsible[a]	Timing or frequency of monitoring[b]
About 32,280 acres of prime farmland would be removed from the county to accommodate future residential and employment growth. **Proposed development would require cancellations and/or Notices of Nonrenewal for Williamson Act Contract Lands**	*Policies* The Growth Accommodation and Agricultural Lands sections of Volume I of the Draft Plan include a number of policies that favour the protection of prime agricultural lands which would serve to partially mitigate the loss of agricultural lands in the County.	Verify inclusion of policies at CPP adoption.	SJCCDD	CPP
	Regulations Developers of agricultural lands could be required to pay an 'impact fee' for each **new unit acre of land developed.** Collected fees could be used to purchase development rights on agricultural land or to support land trusts that purchase conservation easements on farmland. A specific fee structure should be included in the County's Development Title after being adequately studied. **Alternatively, or in conjunction with this mitigation measure, the Development title could require that developers turn over a specific acreage of agricultural lands to an agricultural trust for each acre of land developed**	The SJCCDD should establish an appropriate fee. Payment of these fees should be monitored annually.	SJCCDD	CPP and O (annually)

Table 11.1 *continued*

Impact	Mitigation measures	Monitoring requirements	Person/agency responsible[a]	Timing or frequency of monitoring[b]
	Land use Major changes should occur on the Draft Plan 2010 Map to redesignate areas from residential and commercial/industrial use to agricultural use. Areas within the proposed new/expanded communities, that are not within the early phases of each community should **could** be zoned as Agricultural-Urban Reserve until such time that these lands are needed for development.	Verify change to CPP Land Use map at adoption	SJCCDD	CPP

Source: SJCCDD, 1992

Underlined and bold text refers to the deletions and additions made between the draft and the final EIRs.
a SJCCDD: San Joaquin County Community Development Department
b CPP: Comprehensive Planning Program stage; O: Operational stage

- land-use decisions that have far-reaching implications (such as approval of a general plan for an entire county or city) can be fully evaluated at the earliest possible stage and alternatives considered.

While the above benefits may well outweigh the drawbacks of evaluating land-use plans, it should be noted that many impacts will not be adequately assessed at this level, making it critical that a two-tier approach be applied. Specific developments must undergo some type of environmental analysis, with a focus on impacts not adequately addressed at the general plan stage. In this way, more detailed and site-specific mitigation measures can strengthen those measures applied at a planning level.

As more and more planning and policy documents are evaluated for potential environmental impacts, resource and service agencies will assist in developing appropriate baseline data relevant to this scale of analysis. The skills of biologists, archaeologists, land-use planners and others will be required to both evaluate wide-ranging and site-specific impacts and develop creative, forward-thinking mitigation measures.

Editors' Note: In 1992, the EIR on the San Joaquin County General Plan was awarded the 'Outstanding Environmental Document of the Year' by the Association of Environmental Professionals, California Chapter.

Part IV

SEAs of Policies

12
SEA and the Structural Funds

*Kevin Bradley**

Introduction

This chapter discusses the SEA of the Irish National Plan 1994–1999, a multi-annual, multisectoral regional economic development plan drawn up in accordance with European Union structural funds regulations. The plan was prepared in 1993 and published in September of that year, coinciding with its formal submission to the European Commission. The subsequent Community Support Framework (CSF), which sets out the agreed development priorities, financial allocations, and monitoring and administrative arrangements, was approved by the Commission in July 1994.

The chapter begins with a discussion of the SEA process required for structural funds, and then discusses the development of the Irish National Plan and its SEA as an example of this process.

Structural Funds and Environmental Profiles

The main way in which the European Commission provides financial support for regional development is through the allocation of structural funds under Framework Regulation EEC 2052/88 (European Communities, 1988). An application for funding takes the form of a regional development plan drawn up in partnership between business, local authorities and other interested parties, under the coordination of the appropriate government office. The plans focus on economic development: they establish strategic objectives and the

* The views and observations made in this paper are entirely those of the author and do not necessarily reflect the views of the European Commission.

framework for the future development of the region, and indicate how projects will be selected for future funding.

In 1993, in response to criticism concerning the lack of environmental sensitivity with which it had deployed the first (1989–1993) 'tranche' of structural funds, the Commission amended the Framework Regulation. The new regulation EEC 2081/93 (European Communities, 1993) requires, under articles 8, 9 and 11a, that regional plans submitted under objectives 1, 2 and 5b must include an assessment of their impact on the environment. Objective 1 regions are defined as those whose development is lagging behind (gross domestic product < 75 per cent of the Community average). Objective 2 regions are those suffering from industrial decline. Objective 5b regions concentrate on rural development. The whole of the territory of Ireland is covered by objective 1.

Regulation 2081/93 requires SEAs for regional plans submitted by member states under these objectives to include:

- an appraisal of the environmental situation in the region concerned;
- an evaluation of the impact of the strategies and operations contained in the regional plan in terms of sustainable development, in agreement with Community law in force; and,
- the arrangements made to associate the competent environmental authorities designated by the member state in the preparation and implementation of the operations envisaged in the plan and to ensure compliance with Community environmental rules.

The above is taken as being the basic framework for the evaluation of plans submitted under the relevant objective. However, prior to the council's formal adoption of the revised regulations, the Commission had sent an informal 'aide-mémoire' (European Commission, 1993a) regarding the 'environmental profile' to the member states, as a basis for the formulation of the information required in the environmental appraisal of regional plans. This aide-mémoire provided a degree of elaboration of the basic legislative requirement set out in the regulations, and was ultimately used by the Commission services as the template for its own review exercise of regional plans submitted by the member states. The aide-mémoire stated that the environmental profile for a regional plan should provide an overview of the most significant environmental issues and the most acute environmental problems of a region. Consistent with the wider development plan for each region, the assessment should focus on strategic issues to be taken into account in negotiations between the member state and the Commission for the CSFs.

The Commission proposed that the information arising from this environmental profile be presented in three sections. The first would describe the current environmental situation and key environmental issues in the region concerned. The second would examine the legal and administrative framework with respect to environmental management institutions, organisations and procedures in the region. The third would describe the impact of the regional development plan and/or its components on the environment, focusing on expected changes and the degree to which preventive approaches – including analysis of alternatives, and assessment of the plan's impact with reference to the themes and targets of the Fifth Environmental Action Programme (CEC, 1992) – were incorporated in the plan. In practice, the order of presentation of this information tended to be that the third section preceded the second section for ease of preparation and flow of information. Box 12.1 shows extracts from the aide-mémoire, illustrating the level of detail required.

The SEA Process for Structural Funds

The structural funds process is composed of six stages:

1. preparation of regional plans and environmental profiles by the member states concerned;
2. evaluation of the regional plans and environmental profiles by the Commission in accordance with the requirements of the structural funds regulations;
3. bilateral negotiations between the Commission and the member state or region concerned;
4. the completion of a CSF or Single Programming Document (SPD)*;
5. definition of the forms of intervention; and
6. monitoring and evaluation.

The environmental profile discussed above is part of the first stage, and subsequently informs, and evolves through, the other five stages. The entirety of the environmental analyses, discussions and negotiations taking place throughout these six stages form the SEA process for structural funds. The environmental profile is essentially the first SEA report, and the CSF of stage 4 includes the second SEA report. The following discussion reviews the SEA process for structural funds.

Preparation of Regional Plans and Environmental Profiles

Box 12.2 summarises the structure of the regional plans. Member states provide information on the state of their environment and the expected environmental impacts resulting from the development priorities chosen for their region, in terms of sustainable development and the Community laws in

---

* A CSF is a broad-based document which focuses on the priorities and objectives involved in the allocation of funds. This is then implemented through operational programmes, which are more specific, multiannual financing plans. An SPD combines both the CSF and operational programmes into one document.

Box 12.1 *Extracts from the Aide Mémoire on Environmental Profiles Sent to the Member States for the Preparation of an Environmental Assessment of their Regional Development Plans in the Context of the Structural Funds Regulations*

Key environmental issues
The description should, as far as possible, cover (with the aid, as appropriate, of a map or maps and quantified indicators):
* the location of zones of special environmental interest, distinguishing between those which have a protected status and others;
* the nature and location of acute problems of pollution and the population affected. Problems might be considered acute where there is :
    − pollution in excess of standards laid down by Community legislation where appropriate; or
    − potentially irreversible damage to the environment; or
    − a serious health hazard.
* problems and/or areas of serious stress on the ecosystem, for example with reference to water (quality and quantity), soil quality, deforestation.

The legal and administrative framework
This section should describe briefly:
* the legal and administrative framework within which (i) zones of special environmental interest are designated and protected; and (ii) the regional development plan and environmental policies are coordinated, notably by means of land-use planning, and through the process of project design, approval and implementation;
* The role of the environmental authorities in the planning and implementation of regional development plans.

Impact of regional development plans on the environment
This section should describe:
* the expected change (with specific reference to reduction) in (i) acute problems of pollution and (ii) stress on the ecosystem, (quantified estimates where possible), as a result of actions foreseen under the Regional Development Plan;
* whether, and if so how, preventive action (including analysis of options) is incorporated in the development and design of:
    − major infrastructure networks and projects;
    − regional aid schemes.

Source: European Commission, 1993a

force (articles 8, 9 and 11a of Regulation 2081/93). The Commission provides an aide-mémoire which provides pro forma guidance on complying with the regulatory requirements. Environmental authorities in the member states are associated in the preparation of the plans.

Box 12.2 *Structure of Regional Plans (1994–1999)*

1. Economic and social analysis of the region
2. Description of the environmental situation
3. Results of the previous CSF, finances mobilised, etc
4. Description of strategies to attain objectives of the funds, and priority development axes chosen
5. Specified objectives of each axis, quantified where possible
6. Expected impact of the plan and measures, including their impact on the environment
7. Ex ante evaluation of the information provided
8. Financial table and other information as appropriate, including the role of the environmental authorities in the preparation and implementation of the plan and its proposed measures

Evaluation of Plans and Environmental Profiles

The Commission carries out a systematic evaluation of the plan in the form of a standardised evaluation grid (European Commission, 1993b) based on the requirements of the regulations and the guidance provided in the aide-mémoire. The appraisal grid is accompanied by information for the reviewer in relation to each question, so that they can determine whether or not the environmental profile is complete or not, and which issues need to be focused on in subsequent negotiations with the national authorities concerned.

For example, in evaluating the environmental impact of the strategy and priorities within a regional plan in terms of sustainable development (defined for this exercise with reference to the principal objectives of the Community Fifth Environmental Action Programme (CEC, 1992)), the approach adopted is to examine the key development priorities (energy, transport, tourism, agriculture and industry) to determine to what extent the environmental dimension has been integrated within the overall strategy for each priority. In regard to industry, for instance, the focus is on the extent to which the preventive approach is being pursued by the incorporation or encouragement of more efficient and cleaner production processes, energy efficiency and waste minimisation. For transport the issue is whether or not there exists a national or regional framework for transport policy and management which incorporates both demand and supply-side factors.

Box 12.3 shows an extract from this appraisal grid. Gaps and lacunae in information on the state of the environment, the impact of proposed priorities or the role of the environmental authorities are identified.

Box 12.3 *Extract from Standardized Environmental Appraisal Grid used for the Review of Regional Plans*

Appraisal of existing environmental situation [3.1(a)]:

- **Does it exist?**yes/no
- **Is it comprehensive** in addressing the key environmental issues in the region? yes/no

Location of zones of special interest [3.1(a) – including maps, tables]:

Nature and location of acute problems of pollution and the population affected [3.1(b)]:

Problems and/or stress on the ecosystem [3.1(c)]:

Source: European Commission, 1993a

Bilateral Negotiations

The Directorate-General for Environment, Nuclear Safety and Civil Protection (DGXI) is then involved in drawing up the negotiating mandate for the subsequent CSF; Box 12.4 shows the contents of a CSF. DGXI is also involved in bilateral discussions with the member state and/or regional authorities regarding the environmental impact of the plan, based on the results of the stage 2 evaluations. These negotiations include not only those authorities responsible for the environment, but also those responsible for the various development priorities chosen by the member state and/or region.

Completion of a CSF

The environment is considered at this stage through:

- definition of other environmental and sustainability indicators and objectives for the CSF in general and, where appropriate, for the individual priority axes. An example could be 'to strengthen the economic attractions of the region, dereliction and pollution must be cleaned up and the built environment enhanced. The overall aim is to encourage strong progress towards sustainable development';
- the definition of environmental indicators linked to environmental infrastructure investment. For instance, for programmes related to waste management, an indicator might be 'per cent of municipal solid waste treated' or 'number of local authorities reaching their 25 per cent recycling target';

Box 12.4 *Content of a Community Support Framework*

- A statement of priorities (quantified where possible) for action in relation to consistency with the economic and social policies of the member state and/or region concerned; the economic prospects for the region concerning expected effects and synergies; consistency with other Community policies, including environmental policies.
- An outline of the proposed forms of assistance, which can be:
    - Operational programmes: a series of multi-annual measures which implement the structural fund programme. For instance, measures for the development of indigenous enterprise and local business could include premises for the development of small- and medium-sized enterprises, support for the specific training needs of those enterprises, or incentives for local business investment;
    - large projects (>15 million ECU for productive investment and >25 MECU for infrastructure investment);
    - global grants: multiannual grants of assistance for specific measures managed by a designated intermediary; and/or
    - aid schemes: Community co-financing of aid schemes operated by the member state.
- An indicative financing plan.
- Means for technical assistance, studies, etc., linked to the preparation or implementation of measures.
- Implementing procedures, including monitoring and assessment procedures, and organisational issues.

- definition of general implementation provisions including the role of the member state environmental authorities in the implementation of the CSF within the region concerned; and
- definition of monitoring and evaluation procedures.

In addition, a new standard clause is included, which relates to the need to ensure compliance with Community environmental legislation for all structural funds interventions. This clause requires, inter alia, that:

- measures co-financed by the structural funds must abide by the principles and objectives of the Fifth Environmental Action Programme (CEC, 1992) as well as complying with Community environmental laws in force;
- for operational programmes (see Box 12.4) or other similar operations likely to have a significant impact on the environment, the member states will enclose with their applications for assistance information to enable the Commission to evaluate the impact on the environment; and
- for large projects, either stand-alone or within an operational programme, the application for assistance must be accompanied by a questionnaire on the assessment of the environmental impact of the project concerned

pursuant to Directive 85/337/EEC on project environmental impact assessment (European Communities, 1985).

The above standard requirements represent a form of high-level environmental mitigation, and are the basis for specifying individual mitigation measures within operational programmes. These mitigation measures nearly always take the form of environmental eligibility criteria attached to individual measures (in particular those of an infrastructure nature) within an operational programme. In other words, the project applicant would have to comply with this requirement before grant assistance could be considered. The most common criterion used states that 'where the proposed work(s) require planning and other statutory approvals, such permission(s) must be obtained prior to commencement of any works. Evidence of same should be available to the administering agencies.' This criterion is now incorporated into all information and assistance application forms, where appropriate, so that the potential developer is immediately aware that no grant assistance is available without the necessary statutory procedures being complied with.

Defining the Forms of Intervention

These include operational programmes, large projects, global grants, and aid schemes (see Box 12.4). Operational programmes go through an 'environmental screening' stage, in particular the specific implementing criteria and procedures of the individual measures related to the environmental situation, the state of implementation of Community environmental legislation, and the institutional and administrative arrangements for environmental management in the member state and/or region. For large projects, the Commission has modified the standard application form relating to EIA procedures and sensitive areas (linked to the Birds and Habitats Directives and the Berne Convention).

Monitoring and Evaluation

Member state environmental authorities are involved in monitoring the environmental impact of each of the development priorities within a given CSF, and are responsible for ensuring that Community environmental legislation is respected in the implementation of the CSF.

SEA of the Irish National Plan

The Irish National Plan 1994–1999 (Government of Ireland, 1993) was drawn up by the Department of Finance in co-operation with other departments of the Irish government. The development sectors covered included transport infrastructures, environment infrastructures, agricultural and rural develop-ment, human resources, tourism, energy and telecommunications, local development, fisheries and industry.

Preparation of the Regional Plan and Environmental Profile

The Irish environmental profile for inclusion within the national plan was pre-pared by the Department of the Environment in co-operation with other government departments and statutory agencies. Its objectives were to ensure compliance with the structural funds regulations as amended, and to provide the Commission with the necessary information with which to evaluate the strategic impact of the plan and its development priorities.

The identification and scoping of impacts and the description of the base-line situation followed the model set out in the Commission's aide-mémoire. The procedures and methodology for prediction of likely impacts were ad hoc in nature, relying in the main on published studies and reports on either the state of the environment, or on the impact of certain economic sectors on the environment. In addition, developing environmental policy initiatives were fed into the development of the environmental profile with reference to how the implementation of many of the development sectors would be miti-gated. The final environmental profile for the national plan was drawn together in a single chapter of the plan, which in nine pages gave a strategic overview of the environmental situation, the likely impact of the proposed development priorities, and a description of the legal and administrative framework in regard to environmental management in Ireland. Box 12.5 gives examples from these sections.

Evaluation of the Plan and Environmental Profile

Following formal submission of the Irish National Plan to the Commission in September 1993, DGXI began work on reviewing the environmental profile, as well as the plan itself, using the standardised 'environmental appraisal grid'. The review revealed:

- a good overview of the environmental situation in terms of the key problems of water pollution and waste;
- a number of key environmental impacts associated with certain development sectors, for instance diffuse source pollution associated with agriculture;
- in terms of sustainable development, a lack of information or detail for the five key economic sectors;
- that the preventive approach is being increasingly incorporated into all levels of government and its agencies; and
- a lack of specific detail in relation to the role the environmental

Box 12.5 *Extracts from the Irish Environmental Profile*

Current environmental situation: air quality
'National air quality standards, reflecting similar EC standards, are in force for smoke, sulphur dioxide, nitrogen dioxide and lead. Only in the case of smoke, and for certain locations in Dublin, have these air quality standards been exceeded at any time. Measures taken from September 1990 under the Environment Action Programme to restrict the marketing of bituminous coal in Dublin have been successful; there have been no breaches of air quality standards since that time.

Significant smoke levels, although within the national standards, have been experienced in Cork and a review of the position there has been completed with a view to applying appropriate control measures. A review of air quality in Ireland over the ten year period, 1981-1991, was published by the Environmental Research Unit in July 1993. This confirms that acidification and industrial/transport related forms of air pollution do not at present pose significant problems. Ireland's air quality is generally good and a range of measures is being pursued to maintain this quality and to meet national and international emissions standards in the transport and energy sectors.'

Impact of plan on the environment: agriculture
'Agriculture has impacted on the environment in a number of ways. More intensive stock farming has brought about excessive nutrient enrichment of some waters, particularly by nitrogen and phosphates. Intensive grazing (particularly related to increased sheep numbers) has created a risk of soil erosion in some hill areas and change in the nature and range of vegetative species. Measures to combat farmyard pollution included in the last OP (previous Operational Programme 1989–1993) will be continued under new agri-environment schemes over the period 1994–1999. Agriculture-related water pollution and fish kills have also been significantly controlled by regulatory, educational and investment measures. Further measures in this area will be introduced in relation to nutrient management on farms to reduce further impact on the environment. Directive 91/676/EEC on the protection of waters from pollution by nitrates from agricultural sources is accompanied by a code of good agricultural practice to deal with nitrate losses to ground and surface waters.'

Legal and administrative framework: pollution
'More recent environmental planning and control systems have been developed separately in relation to water pollution, air pollution and waste. While legislation on water and air is comprehensive and adequate, the legislative framework for waste management is not sufficiently developed. The Government is committed to introducing comprehensive legislation on waste and this is now being urgently prepared.

Recently enacted legislation will required the Environmental Protection Agency to license specified activities of major pollution potential on the basis of integrated pollution control; for the activities concerned, this system will replace the single medium control systems described above. In this context, the Agency must have regard, inter alia, to the need to promote sustainable and environmentally sound development processes and operations. All environmental licensing systems embody the possibility, or where necessary the requirement, of reviewing licenses in the light of monitoring information or changes of circumstances after a development has commenced operations.'

authorities would play during the implementation of the plan and its priorities.

On the basis of the above review, DGXI prepared a text for inclusion within the Commission's CSF negotiating mandate with the Irish authorities, setting out its views on what further information would be required in order to better understand and assess the environmental impact of the plan and its sectoral priorities, as well as ensuring full regulatory compliance.

Concurrent with the beginning of the CSF negotiations, the Irish authorities began sending their proposed operational programmes for each of the development priorities described in the plan itself. These documents set out in greater detail the objectives, strategies, specific measures and administrative means by which an individual development priority will be implemented. The operational programme proposals assisted DGXI in its analysis of the impacts of individual development sectors, and provided a good basis for constructive dialogue with the Irish authorities, resulting in amendments in certain cases to the means of implementation in order to avoid potential environmental impacts.

Preparation of the CSF; Defining the Forms of Intervention

The negotiation phase for the Irish CSF lasted approximately six months. During this time, DGXI sought to clarify as much as it could the environmental impact of the national plan and its development priorities. By the end of the process, a CSF document was produced which contained a revised description of the current environmental situation, a description of the likely impact of the proposed development priorities and mitigation measures where appropriate, a set of priority environmental objectives to be achieved in the context of the implementation of the CSF, arrangements for the association of the designated competent environmental authorities in the implementation of the development priorities, and the standard clause regarding the protection of the environment during the implementation of the CSF.

Monitoring and Evaluation

The Irish CSF (European Commission, 1994) was formally adopted by the Commission on 17 July 1994, and is now being implemented. In addition, nine operational programmes have been approved, reflecting the key development priorities described originally in the national plan and now within the CSF. Monitoring of the progress of the CSF and the operational programmes is accomplished through a series of monitoring committees: one for the CSF proper and one each for the individual operational programmes. Their membership includes a designated environmental authority, usually the Department of the Environment, and their duties include ensuring that measures co-financed by the funds are compatible with Community environmental policy.

The Commission, and DGXI in particular, continues to closely monitor the implementation of the CSF and the operational programmes, and is in the process of setting up a formalised reporting procedure whereby ongoing environmental monitoring can be carried out in cooperation with the Irish authorities.

Conclusions

The important regulatory changes in the structural funds programming process, introducing a form of SEA for regional economic development plans, has resulted in much improved CSFs being drawn up, for which the Irish case, described above, is a good example. The process itself has greatly enhanced integration of sustainable development principles within economic development, and shows that it is possible to deal with economic and environmental issues simultaneously.

Further improvements to the process are not likely before 1999, when the existing programming period comes to an end. However, useful lessons have been learnt in regard to the need for more quantification of basic information on the state of the environment within a region and how to present this synoptically, better development sector appraisals in order to identify the most significant environmental impacts associated with them, and awareness raising and training for those within individual development sectors responsible for drawing up strategies and operational programmes so that they are 'sensitised' to environmental issues relevant to their sector.

13

SEA: A Case Study of Follow-up to Canadian Crop Insurance

*Ian Campbell**

In 1994, the Canadian government's Ministry of Agriculture published *Environmental Assessment of Crop Insurance* (Fox and von Massow, 1994). This chapter describes the legislative situation that led to this analysis, its methodology and results, and implications for future policy and programme assessments.

What is Crop Insurance?

Government-assisted crop insurance is an important component of agricultural policy in Canada and many other countries. Agricultural production, particularly cultivated crops, is subject to high variability due to natural hazards, such as drought, hail and pest damage. In order to reduce the risk of natural hazards, governments may partially or fully subsidise crop insurance. In Canada, the federal-provincial Crop Insurance Programme has protected farmers against these yield losses by offering insurance that guarantees revenues equivalent to a minimum yield. The programme is partially subsidised, with producers paying for half of the premium, and federal and provincial governments sharing the other half.

Crop insurance is available for major crops in all provinces. It is not available for some small-scale crops. Participation rates vary widely across crops, provinces and years, from under 10 per cent to over 90 per cent. For major prairie grains, between 50 and 70 per cent of producers participate. In order to qualify for indemnities, field staff from the programme verify that producers

---

* The views expressed in this chapter are those of the author, and do not necessarily represent those of Agriculture and Agri-Food Canada. The author acknowledges valuable suggestions from Carole Martin, Richard Hill and Kathleen Fischer.

have followed good management practices in raising their crops. Standards for good practices vary with crop and local conditions, and are updated periodically. Minimum yields are based on historic yield data. The yield data may be based on the particular plot of land insured, or on average yields in the area.

Legislative Situation: Why Was an Environmental Assessment Done?

The Federal-Provincial Crop Insurance Programme is authorised under enabling legislation called the Farm Income Protection Act (FIPA), passed in 1991. FIPA contains specific clauses requiring EAs. Any programme enacted under FIPA must:

> *require an environmental assessment of the programme to be conducted within two years after the coming into force of the agreement and every five years thereafter, and provide for the manner in which the assessment is to be conducted.*

The environmental requirements in FIPA arose in response to increased awareness of the potential environmental implications of agricultural programmes. In 1990, the federal government made a commitment to consider environmental factors in decisions on new policy and programme proposals. During the development of the FIPA in 1991, the department of agriculture ensured that in addition to an initial EA, periodic re-assessments would be done on existing programmes.

Projects dependent on federal support or approval are subject to a detailed process of EA, review, consultation and mitigation. Procedures vary according to the project. These assessments were governed by the Environmental Assessment and Review Process (EARP) until 1994, and are now governed by the Canadian Environmental Assessment Act (CEAA).

Policies and programmes are exempted from this process, but are required to be assessed for their anticipated environmental impacts. FIPA made specific reference to the need for EAs, as noted above. In contrast to the requirements for assessing projects, the requirements for assessments of policies and programmes do not specify details of the assessment process.

The EA of crop insurance published in 1994 was the first assessment of the federal-provincial crop insurance programme, as required under the act. FIPA is the most important economic legislation affecting the agricultural sector in Canada. In addition to crop insurance, FIPA has required EAs of two other programmes, the Gross Revenue Insurance Programme and the Net Income Stabilisation Fund. These programmes aim mainly to reduce the risk of fluctuating markets, in contrast to crop insurance which reduces the risk of natural hazards.

The EAs in FIPA are required after the programme has been initiated, not during the development stage. The information in the assessment provides guidance on whether the programme should continue, and what modifications would improve its impact on the environment.

The federal Department of Agriculture and Agri-Food is responsible for executing the assessment within its resources. The department is held accountable for the fulfilment of its obligations under FIPA through general accountability mechanisms, including public scrutiny, Access to Information legislation and reports of the auditor general. In the case of crop insurance, the assessment was prepared for the department externally by Price Waterhouse Consultants.

Framework Used for Policy Assessment

Environmental assessments of policies or programmes are more complex than assessments of projects. Policies generally have no direct impact on the environment, but can have secondary effects by changing the decisions of agricultural producers regarding the choice of land, choice of crop, inputs used and tillage methods chosen. These choices can in turn affect the environment. Secondary effects are more difficult to measure than the direct effects of a project.

The subsidisation of crop insurance fulfils the policy objective of protecting producers from natural hazards, but may cause environmental damages if it encourages cultivation of marginal land or other unsustainable practices. Off-farm environmental assets damaged as a result of agriculture are not usually paid for by producers. Ownership and exchanges in public environmental goods rarely exist.

Policies can have different environmental effects in different regions, leading to questions of equity in the distribution of positive and negative effects. A further complication is that policies may improve one environmental attribute, while degrading another. For example, if farmers respond to a policy by relying less on chemical weed control and more on tillage, gains in groundwater quality may be offset by losses in topsoil and surface water quality.

A framework for policy analysis was established to guide the crop insurance assessment through these challenges, as illustrated in Figure 13.1. The assessment evaluates the primary impact of production, the secondary impact on farm and off-farm resources, and the valuation of secondary impacts for society. Assessment tools, such as farm models, are available to address the first phase of this framework. Some research is available to address the second phase, such as fate and transport models for water contaminants. Very few tools are currently available for the third phase, which complicates the assessment of trade-offs between different effects.

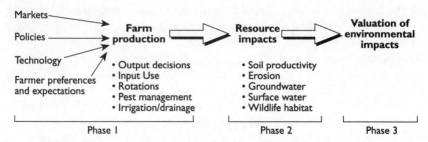

Figure 13.1 *Three Phases in the Evaluation of Environmental Effects of Agricultural Policies*

Purpose and Methodology

The objective of the assessment was to determine what environmental impacts could be attributed to the existence, structure or delivery of crop insurance. In the assessment, all possible alternatives were implicitly considered, including the alternative of no adoption of such specific insurance. In order to isolate the effects of crop insurance, the assessment assumed that all other agricultural programmes would continue to exist.

The assessment drew information from four main sources. A literature review summarised the theoretical and empirical research on crop insurance and the environmental impacts of agriculture. Primary research analysed data from all provinces on crop insurance and its relationship to land use, inputs and other factors. Economic models of farm decisions were used to empirically test the impact of crop insurance on producer behaviour in the context of other signals. Consultations and written submissions from industry stakeholders provided important qualitative insights to the assessment. The project team used a steering committee, including provincial programme managers, to identify key issues and guide the assessment.

The impacts of crop insurance on producer decisions were divided into three categories. First, overall risk reduction included changes in the total production and income risk due to the existence of the programme. Second, relative risk reduction included changes in the relative risk of different crops, land, practices etc. Third, management practices required included the impact of requirements for specific practices for eligibility for the programme.

The project team identified nine key issues:

1 Does the risk reduction from crop insurance affect the crop mix selected?
2 Do crop insurance provisions encourage or discourage innovative land stewardship practices?
3 Does crop insurance affect input use in crop production?
4 Does crop insurance affect the nature of crop rotations?
5 Does crop insurance encourage production using marginal land?

6 Are the 'good farming practices' provisions of crop insurance contracts affecting producer production decisions?

7 Does crop insurance affect the area and type of summerfallow used?

8 Does crop insurance affect the quantity and quality of wildlife habitat?

9 Does crop insurance encourage or discourage organic production?*

In addition to addressing these specific issues, the study analysed how crop insurance fits within the broad context of market signals and government programmes that influence producer decisions.

Each of these issues involves a producer decision that could, in theory, be affected by crop insurance, and that could impact on the environment. The theoretical impacts were tested against empirical evidence to reach conclusions on environmental impacts. Conclusions were drawn where different sources of information on an issue pointed in the same direction. The assessment dealt with scientific and economic uncertainties by searching for consistency and consensus among the sources of information available. Where uncertainties remained, needs for further information were identified. The results were reviewed by programme specialists and environmental analysts at federal and provincial levels.

The analysis took into account potential differences in effect between provinces and between crops. The crop insurance programme applies across a wide variety of environmental landscapes of Canada, from humid coastal zones to the arid Canadian prairies. Each zone has its own agricultural practices and environmental issues. Furthermore, crop insurance programmes vary between different provinces of Canada, leading to potential differences in producer reactions to the programme.

No attempt was made to combine the different impacts into an overall indicator of whether the programme had a positive or negative impact on the environment as a whole. The assessment included specific recommendations on how the programme could be improved to decrease negative impacts and enhance environmental quality.

Results

In general, the assessment found that there is little environmental impact directly attributable to crop insurance. On the nine key issues noted above, the assessment led to the following conclusions:

1 *Crop selection:* The assessment found that market signals and other programmes generally overwhelm any impact of crop insurance on crop

---

* Organic production may or may not be better for the environment. For example, using tillage rather than pestcides to control weeds may decrease the risk of pesticides leaching to surface water, but increase the level of soil erosion.

selection, indicating that there is no significant impact on the environment. However, crop insurance seems to favour potatoes over other crops in the maritime provinces, and grains over forages in the prairie provinces. These influences could have small negative impacts on soil erosion and consequent damage to water quality if good farming practices are not employed.

2 *Land stewardship practices:* The security provided by crop insurance probably has a positive impact on the adoption of sustainable land stewardship practices. By lowering risk, producers are less prone to discount future earnings from the land, and more prone to maintain soil health and productivity.

3 *Input use:* Crop insurance may play a small role in the decision-making process for inputs, but there is no consistent evidence that it increases or decreases input use.

4 *Crop rotations:* Crop insurance was found to provide a small incentive to shorten the rotation in potato production. More frequent planting of potatoes may lead to more soil erosion and input use relative to other crops in a potato rotation.

5 *Marginal land:* The study found no quantitative evidence that crop insurance in particular causes production on marginal land. The cumulative effect of all agricultural support programmes, including crop insurance, may cause environmentally sensitive land to be put into production of annual crops.

6 *Good farming practices:* As currently administered, crop insurance does not seem to enhance or damage the environment through its requirements for good farming practices. The practices required by crop insurance are generally aimed at maintaining yields, which may or may not coincide with good environmental practices.

7 *Summerfallow:* Over the long term, crop insurance was found to provide a larger benefit for grains planted on stubble land than for grains planted on summerfallow. Summerfallow, or leaving a field bare for a season, is used in arid regions to conserve soil moisture for the next season. Summerfallow has a higher risk of soil degradation than planting continuous grain crops.

8 *Wildlife habitat:* The assessment found no evidence that crop insurance provided an incentive to bring wildlife habitat into production. Crop insurance often includes specific provisions to compensate for damage to crops from wildlife.

9 *Organic production:* The lack of comprehensive coverage specifically targeted at organic producers may discourage some producers from organic production. While organic producers may participate in crop insurance, some organic management practices may not be incorporated into crop insurance regimes.

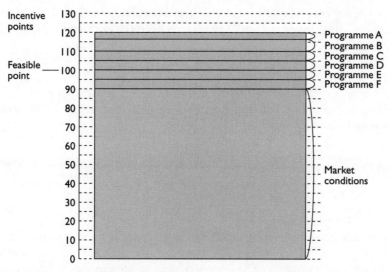

Figure 13.2 *Incentives in Production Decision*

In a broader policy context, the assessment noted that producers make decisions based on a range of signals, including market prices, price stabilisation programmes, fuel tax rebates, transportation subsidies and other factors as well as crop insurance. The cumulative effect of these programmes is illustrated in Figure 13.2. Other programmes may provide incentives to remove land from crops, such as the Permanent Cover Programme in Canada, which offers long-term incentives to shift sensitive prairie land into perennial cover crops.

Any one programme may have a negligible effect, but the cumulative effect of all programmes may affect producer behaviour. Together, they may provide sufficient incentive to move production above the 'feasible' level in Figure 13.2, and cause marginal land to be broken for annual crops, or input use to be raised.

Recommendations

The assessment identified opportunities for overcoming potential problems or seizing opportunities to improve environmental sustainability in the sector through adjustments in the crop insurance programme.

Good Farming Practices

The assessment recommended incorporation of environmentally sound practices into the programme's operations as the best lever to ensure that crop insurance does not contribute to environmental harm. For example, marginal land could be made ineligible for coverage, or incentives could be provided for producers using erosion control or other good farming practices. Good farming practices must be clearly defined, taking into account both environmental and insurance viability.

Individual Coverage
The assessment recommended that individual coverage be adopted as quickly as feasible, as it allows more opportunity for innovation and a more accurate reflection of individual risks.

Organic Production
The assessment recommended attempts to improve provisions for organic production.

Wildlife and Waterfowl Coverage
Improvements in coverage for wildlife and waterfowl damage were recommended. A high level of coverage for damage by wildlife could support a broadly-based societal choice to encourage the maintenance of wildlife habitat.

Testing of New Provisions
All significant alterations to the provisions of the programme were recommended to be tested for environmental soundness. These provisions could be tested using the analytic approach developed in the EA of crop insurance.

Requirements for Ongoing Monitoring
Priority indicators on environmental performance and producer practices should be identified and monitored to improve the EA process. For example, formal definitions of environmentally sensitive land or wildlife habitat could be developed and monitored. They could be used to measure the state of the environment and the impact of all policies.

Comprehensive Approach
The assessment recommended developing a framework for reviewing the impact of agricultural policies in a comprehensive manner, in order to determine the total effect of programmes and the interaction between programmes.

Impact of the Assessment

The assessment was made available to the public, and distributed to provincial, federal and producer stakeholders concerned with crop insurance or the environmental impacts of agricultural policy. This fulfilled the requirements of the FIPA regarding assessment of the programme's environmental impact. Since the assessment found that the programme generally had little effect on the environment, there was no need for immediate action.

The recommendations did point out programme refinements that would enhance its environmental impact. It is too early to tell how many of these recommendations will eventually be incorporated in the programme. The EA was distributed to federal and provincial officials responsible for crop insurance. The crop insurance programme is undergoing an in-depth review in 1995 and 1996, with a view to introducing modifications to the programme in 1997. The recommendations of the EA report will be considered in the review, along with other aspects of the programme. The fact that such an EA has been done increases the chances of incorporating environmental factors in the programme design.

Two of the recommendations of the report deal with issues beyond the crop insurance programme itself. These recommendations have been echoed in other reports, and are being acted on:

- The recommendation for ongoing monitoring supports the need for environmental indicators to monitor the impact of agricultural activity on the environment. The Canadian government is investing resources in creating a set of environmental indicators relevant to agricultural policy, in consultation with the agri-food sector, agronomists and scientists, and in coordination with international bodies (McRae, 1995).
- The recommendation for a comprehensive approach to analysing the environmental impact of agricultural policies is being addressed with better analytic tools and more comprehensive processes. Agriculture and Agri-Food Canada has developed a model to evaluate the overall impact of agricultural policies on soil erosion in the prairie region (Bouzaher et al, 1995). All departments of the Canadian government are currently preparing sustainable development strategies which will address the full range of their activities, policies and programmes. Work is under way in the department to analyse the total set of market and policy signals.

The environmental assessment of crop insurance provides a framework that can be used to evaluate a wide range of agricultural policies.

Lessons Learned

The environmental requirement included in the FIPA ensured that a systematic assessment of environmental issues was included in the policy review process. This process confirmed that the programme would not cause significant environmental damage, and raised the probability of future improvements.

Policy assessments raise complicated issues of social equity that go beyond issues of the physical environment. A policy can have positive impacts on one environmental factor while damaging another. It is sometimes difficult to define environmentally sound practices due to trade-offs between different environmental factors. For example, weed control with tillage may increase soil erosion, while weed control with pesticides may increase damage to water quality.

EAs of policies and programmes have a higher level of uncertainty than assessments of projects. Policy assessments deal with unpredictable human behaviour spread over different regions, in addition to the scientific unknowns associated with any EA.

Policy assessments provide the opportunity for recommendations to go beyond mitigating the impacts of the policy under question. For example, society's desire for more wildlife habitat can be expressed in enhanced crop insurance benefits for wildlife damage, even though crop insurance itself has no effect on habitat. Individual policy assessments would be improved if they could be analysed in the context of the total set of market and policy signals.

Part V

_____

Conclusions

_____

14
Learning from SEA Practice

Maria Rosário Partidário and Riki Thérivel

The cases studies of Chapters 4–13 exemplify a wide range of approaches to SEA, including methods and techniques used in practice. Each of the case studies demonstrates aspects of good practice, but also difficulties and limitations. This chapter focuses on key issues emerging from current SEA practices, the costs and benefits of SEA, and future directions. Although these issues have already been discussed in a theoretical context elsewhere (eg Partidário, 1996), the interesting aspect here is that they are referred to as a result of the application of SEA principles and methodologies in practice. As such, these points can act as a reservoir of experience from which those wishing to learn from practice can draw.

Key Issues in the Practice of SEA

Key issues in SEA practice include SEA regulations and guidelines; links between SEA and sustainable development, PPP decision-making, other SEAs and project EIAs; SEA methodology; and the role of interest groups.

SEA Regulations and Guidelines

Most SEAs are still being carried out on a voluntary basis, usually by public bodies. These SEAs are sometimes supported by guidelines (eg the UK and Canada), but only in a few countries (eg the US and the Netherlands) are they based on a legal framework.

It is debatable whether the enactment of SEA legislation is the most effective step in initiating the implementation and use of SEA. Only a small proportion of PPPs have a formal authorisation stage (eg comprehensive plans, fiscal programmes) and are thus amenable to the 'incremental' SEA models which feed SEA into the PPP's authorisation stage. The rest are developed in a continuous and flexible manner, with many hidden decisions being taken throughout the process. Forcing some form of SEA-and-authorisation stage on these PPPs would be extremely cumbersome, and would limit the continuous and flexible character that SEA should have in the context of PPP decision-making. SEA should be a flexible tool which is used throughout PPP-making, and affects the many small, incremental decisions taken throughout PPP-making, not just the final authorisation decision.

The sequence of development of SEA regulations, guidelines, methodologies and case studies in practice is arguable. Regulators tend to be unwilling to establish SEA regulations in the absence of generally agreed SEA methodologies, which in turn require testing through case studies. This suggests that more case studies should be carried out before SEA regulations are enacted: it can be argued that a change in approach to PPP-making is needed first; methodologies will then be developed, and regulations and guidelines will reflect these methodologies once they emerge.

On the other hand, the number of SEA case studies is likely to remain low unless SEAs are legally required (or at least strongly encouraged). The British government's publication of SEA guidelines for development plans – which have almost the weight of regulations – has spurred an enormous growth in the number of SEAs prepared, and consequently a rapid development and evolution of SEA methodologies. This could be an argument for 'methodology-forcing', where regulations are enacted despite the lack of agreed methodologies, in the expectation that these methodologies will emerge. (Interestingly, as soon as the UK published a 'good-practice' SEA guidebook which drew from early case studies, methodological innovation virtually ceased, as the great majority of local authorities followed those – and only those – practices shown in the guidebook) (Thérivel, 1995).

At this moment, the development of SEA guidelines may be preferable to that of SEA regulations. Whereas regulations may be held back by legal concerns, guidelines can afford to be more exigent in the promotion of best practice. Once SEA methodologies and approaches have been further developed, regulations can be implemented to reflect this practice.

Links to Sustainability

Most of the case studies link SEA to the principles and objectives of sustainable development. These links include the establishment of sustainability objectives, sustainability indicators and a coherent approach to social, economic, cultural, equity and environmental concerns. The SEA of Hertfordshire's development plan (Chapter 9) is an example of how the principles of sustainability can be integrated into the land-use planning process.

Nevertheless, difficulties exist in establishing linkages with sustainability policies and targets. These include not only the definition of sustainability targets and measurement tools, but also a change in outlook. In particular, links to sustainability involve greater levels of public consultation, which SEA as currently practiced does not encourage.

Links to PPP Decision-Making

The links between SEA and the PPP-making process are difficult to clearly identify and explain, but are crucial to the effectiveness of SEA. Some SEA critics feel that SEA adds little to the PPP-making process, which already sets objectives, considers alternatives and mitigates impacts. Others, instead, are concerned that SEA should not take over decision-making, which is essentially a political process.

The case studies demonstrate that SEA can be a useful tool which improves PPP-making by informing political decisions and helping to build consensus: 'the integration of SEA in the comprehensive planning process can contribute to a general improvement and transformation of both the process and the results' (Chapter 10).

However, SEA can only be effective if decision-makers feel that it is important, otherwise it becomes 'nothing but a paper exercise' (Chapter 5). This may be difficult where the PPP is subject to strong political pressure, or a very long time frame.

To be effective, SEA must start at the earliest stages of PPP-making, before any important decisions are made, and must be integrated throughout PPP-making. This is shown particularly clearly in the Swedish case study (Chapter 10). If SEA is carried out in parallel with PPP-making, it is unlikely to slow the PPP down, or to reduce its flexibility. However, a late SEA, like late-project EIA, may slow down the PPP by raising environmental concerns at a stage when most decisions have already been made. Chapter 8 is probably an example of this: it is uncertain how many of the Nepalese SEA's suggestions will be implemented in the final Bara District forest plan, because the SEA process was clearly separate from the PPP-making process, and carried out quite late in the process. Nevertheless, the SEA still raises useful points which may well be incorporated into the final plan.

Finally, as was highlighted in Chapter 4, there are time problems in developing and agreeing on PPPs: by the time a PPP is operational, new issues and problems may have emerged, and new information may be necessary.

Links to Other SEAs and to Project EIA

Several case studies highlighted the need for coherent links between the various tiers of SEA. For instance, the Dutch waste management example (Chapter 7) identified different roles for SEAs at different tiers: at the national level SEA looks at the impacts of various approaches and options, at the provincial level it looks at alternative locations and capacities, and at the project level it looks at design and mitigation measures. The SEA for the US environmental restoration and waste management programme (Chapter 5) identifies potential sites within a region where future facilities could be located: subsequent EIAs are expected to identify specific sites and mitigate impacts at these sites.

SEAs thus clearly need to 'trickle down' to project EIA. Many SEA recommendations may not be implementable at the strategic level, and may instead need to be put in place at the project level. SEAs can also be an important resource for use at project EIA levels. SEAs will never replace project EIAs, but they can strongly reduce the effort and resources involved in developing project EIAs.

To be effective, the SEA process also needs to begin at the most strategic policy level and 'trickle down' to lower tiers of PPP-making. It may be of little use to require SEAs at lower tiers if a more strategic policy, with a strong influence over subsequent tiers of decision-making (for instance the European Common Agricultural Policy, which influenced most other European agricultural PPPs), has not been subject to SEA. Chapter 6, for instance, recommends that the trans-European rail network should be reappraised within the framework of all proposed measures arising from the European Community transport policy.

SEAs need to consider the implications of other PPPs and other actions and ensure that there are no inconsistencies. For instance, the Hertfordshire case study highlights issues outside the remit of the structure plan which have nevertheless affected the effectiveness of the plan, for instance national road programmes and household projections. SEAs may be difficult to carry out in the face of increasing privatisation of activities formerly carried out by public bodies.

Existing experience shows that different SEAs, EIAs and PPPs are, unfortunately, rarely coordinated and linked. This piecemeal approach to SEA contradicts the generally accepted principle of linking SEAs and EIAs to ensure a sound and broad environmental assessment at a more global scale.

Methodology

SEA techniques and approaches are usually based on those used in project EIA, policy appraisal and planning. Simple methods often seem to be quite successful: for instance, the case studies use zoning (eg German wind farms), maps (trans-European rail network), and matrices (Nepalese forest management) to good effect. On the other hand, more complex techniques such as photomontage, remote sensing and especially GIS are developing rapidly, and are likely to be used increasingly in the future.

SEA techniques can only be successfully applied if the necessary environmental data exist. Several of the case studies recommended that integrated databases be developed, arguing that the availability of appropriate information can substantially reduce the resources needed for, and the duration of, an SEA. For instance, the example of the trans-European rail network showed that, had there been an adequate database, the time needed for the SEA could have been halved.

Few of the case studies show a clear analysis of cumulative impacts, which is something that SEA is supposed to address particularly well. However, in the example of US environmental restoration and waste management, significant cumulative impacts were identified at an early stage, and mitigation measures were applied which related to both policy language and regulatory measures.

The case studies show that SEA is, to an extent, being held back by the heavy inheritance of methodologies from project EIA. SEA must assume its own status and develop more independently of project EIA. More strategically oriented techniques such as compatibility matrices, exclusion zoning, or life-cycle analysis must be developed, particularly for use with higher-tier PPPs. Learning SEA only from EIA may lead to a closed circle, as it will be difficult to find new ideas for SEA based only on existing project EIA processes and methodologies.

Interest Groups

SEA is inherently a complex subject which cannot be approached from only one direction. It involves a wide range of professionals from different disciplines (engineers, ecologists, planners, politicians etc), and requires that they work together. Consultation with a wide range of groups, including the general public, can both enhance and give credence to SEA. Full participation of regional and local authorities can lead to broad acceptance of the SEA results and PPP conclusions.

Some of the case studies show examples of broad collaboration between the various relevant interest groups. For instance, the Swedish example involved extensive dialogue between planners, environmental experts, economics and a wide range of other disciplines. In Hertfordshire, a range of interest groups, including the public, participated in drawing up the plan 'vision' and in carrying out the SEA. For the US environmental restoration and waste management programme, more than 15,000 comments from the public were gathered and analysed. In at least one case, the interest groups provided useful information that otherwise might have taken too long to be collected.

Dialogues such as those discussed in Chapter 10 must be opened up between the interest groups involved, to reduce concerns about the role of SEA in PPP-making, and to gain maximum advantage from SEA. There may be a need to develop particular skills for SEA, particularly the ability to deal with many disciplines.

Costs and Benefits of SEA

The case studies identify a range of costs and benefits associated with the SEA process.

Costs

The time and financial costs of SEA are generally relatively easy to measure, especially if the SEA has been carried out by consultants. For instance, the SEA for the San Joaquin County comprehensive plan cost $623,000 and took several years. That for the trans-European rail network required 40 person-months of work over 10 months. The Dutch SEA study took 10 months. Chapter 5 does not list the SEA cost, but compares SEA to project EIA, which generally costs 0.1–1 per cent of the project costs. Where the SEA process is carried out internally, the costs may be harder to identify, since the SEA may be so closely linked to the PPP-making process that the two are indistinguishable.

Not all SEAs are enormous. Those shown here tend to be particularly good, comprehensive studies, with correspondingly high costs. However, the authors are aware of many small SEAs that have taken less than a week to carry out, and that are still felt to be useful by the PPP-makers (Thérivel, 1995).

Benefits

The benefits of SEA are more intangible. Obviously, the largest benefit is in terms of environmental enhancement or reduction of the environmental harm associated with the PPP. This can be in the form of:

- new approaches to the PPP: for instance, Hertfordshire's entire approach to housing is influenced by the SEA;
- a framework for subsequent PPPs and projects: for example, wind farm proposals in Germany's Soest district are influenced by the SEA for wind farm development in that region;
- specific mitigation measures for the PPP. The SEA for the San Joaquin comprehensive plan lists these mitigation measures specifically, and proposes a programme to monitor their implementation. Chapter 12 shows how structural fund applications can be improved through SEA to include more environmentally benign measures.

Another benefit of SEA can be a reduction in the duration of the authorisation process. For instance, the SEA for German wind farms has led to a significant reduction in the time taken to make decisions on wind farm applications. The Dutch case study considered that SEA did not delay the decision-making process, but instead was useful for the proponent, who has voluntarily decided to carry out another SEA. SEAs can also help to put in place a range of mech-anisms (eg databases, working groups) that ultimately contribute to greater efficiency and flexibility in the PPP processes.

However, SEAs with long-term time horizons risk a lack of sufficient resources. The benefits of these SEAs may only become evident in the long term, and may not be seen as a priority by traditional decision-makers.

One benefit of SEAs which is not yet really emerging in practice is increased transparency and public involvement in decision-making. However, this is likely to be demonstrated once more case studies are available and prac-tice becomes more evident.

Future Directions for the Practice of SEA

This section identifies future directions in SEA arising from SEA practice. Although some of these conclusions may sound relatively obvious, they aim to serve as indicators of likely future change, and an inspiration for those carrying out SEAs.

- SEA is only really effective when it starts early and accompanies the entire PPP process, from its inception through the multiple stages of decision-making.
- SEAs should be linked to sustainability, and should consider all the elements of sustainable development: economic, socio-cultural and biophysical. Trade-off analysis can be used to test various PPP approaches, and to ensure that SEA is not merely a pro forma exercise. Environmental considerations need to be fully considered in decision-making, on a par with financial and socio-economic considerations.
- Realistic SEA objectives and/or 'visions' must be established early on. It may be useful to establish targets or benchmarks against which impacts can later be evaluated, but there may be political and economic difficulties in establishing these targets.
- SEAs should be based on a systematic methodology, possibly linking objectives, indicators, baseline analysis, impact predictions, mitigation and monitoring. SEAs should include a statement of the methods used in carrying out the analysis.
- The consideration of a range of alternatives is a crucial component in SEA, otherwise SEA risks becoming a post hoc exercise which merely justifies an agreed-upon PPP.
- SEA relies on the availability of suitable data: integrated databases need to be developed.
- Simple impact prediction and evaluation techniques are often as useful as, and considerably less resource intensive than, more complex techniques.

New techniques specific to SEA need to be developed, including simple methods for dealing with uncertainty.

- The interest groups involved in SEA – including the public – need more training in SEA techniques, and need to communicate more with one another. Consultation with relevant experts and the public is crucial to SEA. Transparency and legitimacy needs to be encouraged.

Conclusion

SEA is under way. In recent years SEA studies have moved from discussions about the need for SEA to analyses of how practice is contributing to improved SEA effectiveness. This book tries to show what is happening with SEA in various parts of the world. For logistical reasons, it has not covered a number of other interesting case studies. However, the authors hope that the case studies presented here will help to stimulate a wider application of SEA principles, objectives, methodologies and tools.

SEA is becoming an integral element of PPP decision-making practice: not an add-on tool which increases costs and complicates bureaucratic procedures, but a set of principles and objectives that can help to change the way PPP processes are conducted and make them more environmentally sound and sustainable.

References

Chapter 1

Commission of the European Communities (CEC) (1993) *Report from the Commission of the Implementation of Directive 85/337/EEC*, COM(93) 28 Final, Vol 13, Brussels

Department of the Environment (DoE) (1991) *Monitoring Environmental Assessment and Planning*, HMSO, London

Glasson, J, R Thérivel, J Weston, E Wilson and R Frost (1995) *Changes in the Quality of Environmental Statements for Planning Projects*, Final Report, Oxford Brookes University, Oxford

House of Commons Environment Committee (1986) *Planning: Appeals, Call Ins and Major Public Inquiries*, Session 1985–86, Fifth Report, HMSO, London

Lee, N and D Brown (1992) 'Quality Control in Environmental Assessment', *Project Appraisal* 7(1), pp 41–5

Partidário, MR (1992) *An Environmental Assessment and Review (EAR) Procedure: a Contribution to Comprehensive Land-use Planning*, PhD dissertation, University of Aberdeen

Partidário, MR (1994) *Key Issues in Strategic Environmental Assessment*, Final Report, NATO/FEARO research project, Ottawa (unpublished report)

Sheate, W R (1992) 'Strategic Environmental Assessment in the Transport Sector', *Project Appraisal*, September, pp 170–174

Thérivel, R, E Wilson, S Thompson, D Heaney and D Pritchard (1992) *Strategic Environmental Assessment*, Earthscan, London

Thompson, S, J Treweek and D Thurling (1995) 'The potential application of strategic environmental assessment (SEA) to the farming of Atlantic salmon (Salmo salar L) in mainland Scotland', *Journal of Environmental Management* 45, pp 219–229

Wood, C (1995) *Environmental Impact Assessment: A Comparative Review*, Longman, Harlow

Wood, C and M Djeddour (1991) 'Strategic Environmental Assessment: EA of Policies, Plans and Programmes', *The Impact Assessment Bulletin*, 10 (1), pp 3–22

Chapter 2

Australia, Cabinet (1994) *Cabinet Handbook 1994 Edition (Approved Draft)*, Canberra

Australia, Commonwealth Environment Protection Agency (EPA) (1994) *Review of Commonwealth Environmental Impact Assessment: Assessment of Cumulative Impacts and Strategic Assessment in Environmental Impact Assessment*, Canberra

Balfors, B (1994) 'EIA and a General Plan in Sweden: A Case-Study', paper presented at the *Nordic EIA Effectiveness Workshop*, Tuusula (Finland)

Bregha, F, J Bendickson, D Gamble, T Shillington and E Weick (1990) 'The Integration of Environmental Considerations into Government Policy', report prepared for the Canadian Environmental Research Council, Ottawa

Bridgewater, G S (1989) 'Environmental Impact Assessment of Policies in Canada: A Beginning', paper presented at IAIA'89, *8th Annual Meeting of the International Association for Impact Assessment*, Montreal, Québec

Canada, Department of Energy, Mines and Resources (EMR), Office of Environmental Affairs (1994) *EMR's Environmental Screening Procedure Manual*, Draft, Ottawa

Canada, Department of Environment (DOE) (1994) *Environmental Assessment of Policies and Programmes in Environment Canada, Compendium of DOE Information and Procedural Guidance for Environmental Assessment Managers and Policy and Programme Developers*, Draft, Ottawa

Canada, Department of Natural Resources (NRCan) (1993) *Guidelines for the Integration of Environmental Considerations into Energy Policies*, Ottawa

Canada, Federal Environmental Assessment Review Office (1989) *From Project to Policy Assessment: Proceedings of the Canada–The Netherlands Workshop on Environmental Impact Assessment*, Vol 1, Ottawa

Canada, Federal Environmental Assessment Review Office (1992) *Environmental Assessment in Policy and Programme Planning: A Source-book*, Ottawa (unpublished)

Canada, Federal Environmental Assessment Review Office (1993) *The Environmental Assessment Process for Policy and Programme Proposals*, Ottawa

Canada, Federal Environmental Assessment Review Office (1994) *Review of the Implementation of the Cabinet Directive: The Environmental Assessment Process for Policy and Programme Proposals*, Second Draft, Ottawa

Canada, Projet de Société (1994) *Towards a National Sustainable Development Strategy for Canada: Canadian Choices for Transitions to Sustainability*, Vol 5, Ottawa

Canadian International Development Agency (CIDA) (1993) *Guide to Integrating Environmental Considerations into CIDA Policies and Programmes*, Draft, prepared by Resources Future International, Hull

Denmark, Ministry of the Environment, Spatial Planning Department (1994) *Guidance on Procedures for Environmental Assessment of Bills and Other Government Proposals: cf Administrative Order No 31*, English Version Draft, Copenhagen

Dixon, J (1993) 'EIA in Policy and Plans: New Practice in New Zealand', paper presented at the 13th Annual Conference of the International Association of Impact Assessment, Shanghai, China

Dixon, J (1994) 'Strategic Environmental Assessment in New Zealand: A Progress Report', paper presented at the 14th Annual Meeting of the International Association of Impact Assessment, Quebec City, Canada

Dixon, J and T Fookes (1995) 'Environmental Assessment in New Zealand: Prospects and Practical Realities', *Australian Journal of Environmental Management* 2(2), pp 104–111

Elling, B (1994) 'Strategic Assessment in Denmark: Some Results and Perspectives', paper presented at the 14th Annual Meeting of the International Association for Impact Assessment, Quebec City, Canada

European Commission (1994) *Strategic Environmental Assessment: Existing Methodology*, report prepared by DHV Environment and Infrastructure BV for Directorate-General for Environment, Nuclear Safety and Civil Protection, Brussels

Goodland, R and G Tillman (1995) *Strategic Environmental Assessment: Strengthening the Environmental Assessment Process*, Discussion Draft, World Bank, Washington, DC

Holtz, S (1991) 'Issues in the Environmental Assessment of Policy: A Research Prospectus', Canadian Environmental Assessment Research Council, Ottawa, (unpublished)

LeBlanc, P (1994) 'Application of EA to Policies and Programs: The Canadian Experience', paper presented at the Dutch SEA Workshop, The Hague

Lerman, P (1994) 'EIS in Sweden; A Tool for Good Management of Resources' (to be published in *The Environmental Professional*)

Lerman, P (1995) 'Physical Planning Linked to EIA; A Method for Processing Knowledge That Promotes Sustainability and Efficient Procedures', (unpublished)

Netherlands, Advisory Committee on the Environmental Test (ACET) (1993) *Advisory Report of the Committee on the Introduction of an Environmental Test and an Environmental Paragraph for National Government Policy Proposals*, The Hague

Netherlands, General Environmental Policy Division, Directorate for General Policy Affairs (1992) *NEPP Action Point A 141: Strategy and Progress*, The Hague

Netherlands, Ministry of Housing, Physical Planning and Environment (MHPPE) (1989) *National Environmental Policy Plan (NEPP): To Choose or To Lose*, The Hague

Netherlands, Ministry of Housing, Physical Planning and Environment (1990) *National Environmental Policy Plan – Plus (NEPP-Plus)*, The Hague

Partidário, MR (1994) 'Key issues in Strategic Environmental Assessment', NATO/FEARO (unpublished report)

Scott, S (1992) 'Environmental Considerations in Decision-Making: A Role for EIA at the Policy Level?', report prepared for the Canadian Environmental Assessment Research Council, Ottawa

United Kingdom, Cabinet (1994) 'Central Government', in *Sustainable Development: The UK Strategy*, Chapter 29, HMSO, London

United Kingdom, Department of the Environment (DoE) (1991) *Policy Appraisal and the Environment: A Guide for Government Departments*, HMSO, London

United Kingdom, Department of the Environment (1993) *Environmental Appraisal of Development Plans: A Good Practice Guide*, HMSO, London

United Kingdom, Department of the Environment (1994) *Environmental Appraisal in Government Departments*, HMSO, London

Veart, S (1994) 'New Zealand Status Report: Challenges for EIA: Emerging Trends, Issues and Some Innovative Approaches', paper submitted to the Federal Environmental Assessment Review Office, Ottawa (unpublished)

Ward, M (1994) 'Policy Proposal for Discussion: Environmental Assessment of

Government Policy Decisions: Further Steps Towards Sustainability', paper presented at the Canada/Australia/New Zealand Workshop on EA Effectiveness, Canberra

World Bank (1991) *Environmental Assessment Sourcebook*, Vols 1 and 2, Environment Department, Washington DC

World Bank (1993) 'Sectoral Environmental Assessment', *Environmental Assessment Sourcebook Update 4*, Washington, DC

World Bank (1994) *Making Development Sustainable: The World Bank Group and the Environment Fiscal 1994*, Washington, DC

Chapter 3

Commission of the European Communities (1994) *Strategic Environmental Assessment: Existing Methodology*, report to Directorate-General XI

Department of the Environment (DoE) (1989) *Environmental Assessment: A Guide to the Procedures*, HMSO, London

Department of the Environment (1991) *Monitoring Environmental Assessment and Planning*, HMSO, London

Department of the Environment (1993) *Environmental Appraisal of Development Plans: A Good Practice Guide*, HMSO, London

Federal Environmental Assessment Review Office (FEARO) (1995) in Wood, C *Environmental Impact Assessment: A Comparative Review*, Longman, Harlow

Fergusson, M and D Wilkinson (1995) *LGMB Indicators for Sustainable Development: A Step by Step Guide*, Second Draft, IEEP, London

Glasson, J, R Thérivel, J Weston, E Wilson and R Frost (1995) *Changes in the Quality of Environmental Statements for Planning Projects*, Final Report, Oxford Brookes University, Oxford

Local Government Management Board (LGMB) (1996) *Indicators for Local Agenda 21: A Summary*, LGMB, Luton

Partidário, MR (1994) 'EA at Policy and Planning Levels', in *15th International Seminar on Environmental Assessment and Management*, CEMP, Aberdeen

Scottish Office (1994) *Setting Forth: Environmental Appraisal of Alternative Strategies*, Edinburgh

Thérivel, R, E Wilson, S Thompson, D Heaney and D Pritchard (1992) *Strategic Environmental Assessment*, Earthscan, London

US Department of Agriculture (1990) *Final Environmental Impact Statement: Vegetation Management in the Ozark/Ouachita Mountains*, Management Bulletin RB–MB45, Forest Service Southern Region, Atlanta

US Department of the Army (1988) *Chemical Stockpile Disposal Program: Final Programmatic Environmental Impact Statement*, Aberdeen Proving Ground, Maryland

Verheem, R (1992) 'Environmental Assessment at the Strategic Level in the Netherlands', *Project Appraisal 7*, pp 150–156

Verheem, R (1994) 'Case Study: Strategic Environmental Assessment of the Dutch Ten Year Programme on Waste Management', paper presented at the International

Association for Impact Assessment annual conference, Quebec

Wilkinson, D, S Mullard and M Fergusson (1994) *Strategic Environmental Assessment: Implications for the English Countryside*, Countryside Commission

Wood, P (1995) *Towards a Robust Judgement of Significance in EIA*, MSc dissertation, Oxford Brookes University

Chapter 4

ABU (1989) Atlas der Brutvögel des Kreises Soest, Lohne

Braun, R, R Kleinert, C Schmidt et al (1994) 'Ermittlung von Gewerbe-, Industrie- und Wohnbauflächenpotential in Hagen aus der Sicht der Umwelt', *UVP-Report* 8(2), pp 77–81

Bundesministerium für wirtschaftliche Zusammenarbeit (1995) *UVP in der Entwicklungshilfe*, Bonn

German Government (1975) 'Grundsätze für die Prüfung der Umweltverträglichkeit öffentlicher Massnahmen des Bundes vom 12.09.1975', GMBI.S. 717

Hirtz, W, W Huber, V Kleinschmidt, FT Pietzka, and J Heiderich (1991) 'Umweltvorsorgeprüfung bei Forschungsvorhaben', *Zeitschrift für Umweltpolitik und Umweltrecht* 14, pp 179–195

Huber, W and W Hirtz (1992) 'Umweltvorsorgeprüfung bei Forschungsvorhaben – am Beispiel von Photovoltaik – Band 2: Methodische Überlegung zur Umweltvorsorgeprüfung und Darstellung des gewählten Prüfverfahrens', *Berichte des Forschungszentrums Jülich*, Jülich

Hübler, K-H, C Richl, and B Winkler-Kühlken (1995) *Umweltverträglichkeitsprüfung in der Bauleitplanung: Praxisprobleme und Lösungsvorschläge im Auftrag des Umweltbundesamtes und der Europäischen Kommission*, Berlin

Jacoby, C, K Mangels, and J Stuffel (1994) 'UVP-Typen im Spiegel der Planungsdynamik in der Flächennutzungsplanung', *UVP-Report* 8(2), pp 97–101

Jansen, P G and D Wagner (1993) *Catalogue of Criteria for Examining Plans and Programmes in Regional Planning and Laender Development Planning Taking Account of Environmental Aspects*, Federal Environmental Agency, Research and Development Project No 101 02 085, Köln

Kleinschmidt, V (1995) 'Methodology and Research on EIA and SEA in Germany', in European Commission *Environmental Impact Assessment: Methodology and Research*, Third EU Workshop on Environmental Impact Assessment, Delphi, 1994, pp 101–106

Kleinschmidt, V, N Schauerte-Lüke and R Bergman (1994) 'Rahmenkonzept für Windkraftanlagen und -parks im Binnenland: ein Beispiel aus Nordrhein-Westfalen', *Natur und Landschaft* 1, pp 9–18

Wagner, D and V Kleinschmidt (1995) 'Feasibility of a Strategic Environmental Assessment for the German Federal Traffic Infrastructure Plan', in Hughes, J and N Lee *Strategic Environmental Assessment Legislation and Procedures in the Community*, Final Report Vol 2, University of Manchester, Manchester

Chapter 5

Sigal, L L and J W Webb (1989) 'The Programmatic Environmental Impact Statement: Its Purpose and Use', *Environmental Professional* 11, pp 14–24

US Department of Agriculture (USDA) and US Department of Interior (USDOI) (1994) *Final Supplemental Environmental Impact Statement on Management of Habitat for Late-Successional and Old-Growth Forest Related Species Within the Range of the Northern Spotted Owl*, Washington, DC

US Department of Energy (DOE) (1994) *Implementation Plan, Environmental Restoration and Waste Management Programmatic Environmental Impact Statement*, DOE/EIS-0200, Washington, DC

US Department of Energy (1995) *Environmental Restoration and Waste Management Draft Programmatic Environmental Impact Statement*, DOE/EIS-0200 Washington, DC

Webb, J W and L L Sigal (1992) 'Strategic Environmental Assessment in the United States', *Project Appraisal* 7, pp 137–141

Chapter 6

Commission of the European Communities (CEC) (1990) *The European High Speed Train Network*, Brussels

Commission of the European Communities (1992a) *The Future Development of the Common Transport Policy; A Global Approach to the Construction of a Community Framework for Sustainable Mobility*, COM (92)494, Brussels

Commission of the European Communities (1992b) Green Paper on the Impact of Transport on the Environment, COM 92(46), Brussels

Commission of the European Communities (1993a) *Growth, Competitiveness, Employment: The Challenges and Ways into the 21st Century*, Bulletin of the European Communities, Supplement 6/93, Brussels

Commission of the European Communities (1993b) *The European High Speed Train Network: Environmental Impact Assessment, Executive Summary*, Directorate-General VII, Brussels

Commission of the European Communities (1994) *Proposal for a European Parliament and Council Decision on Community Guidelines for the Development of the Trans-European Network*, COM(94) 106, Brussels

Commission of the European Communities (1995) *Amended Proposal for a European Parliament and Council Decision Concerning Guidelines for the Development of the Trans-European Transport Network*, COM (95)298, Brussels

Greenpeace (1995) *Missing Greenlinks*, Vienna-Zürich

Mens en Ruimte (1993) *The European High Speed Train Network: Environmental Impact Assessment*, report to the Commission of the European Communities, Brussels

Ministère de l'Environnement (1994) *Evaluation environnementale des programmes intermodaux de transport*, report prepared by Association Aménagement Environnement, Paris

Royal Society for the Protection of Birds (1995) *The Impact of Trans-European Networks on Nature Conservation: a Pilot Project*, Sandy, Bedfordshire

T&E, European Federation for Transport and Environment (1995) *Ten questions on TENs*, Brussels

Chapter 7

EIA Commission (1992) *Toetsingsadvies over het MER Tien Jaren Programma Afval 1992–2002*, ISBN 90-5237–350–7, The Netherlands

VROM (1992) 'Towards a Ten Year Programme on Waste Management: Dutch Waste Management Council', proceedings of the Netherlands-Canada Workshop on EIA, The Netherlands, pp 195–243

Waste Management Council (WMC) (1992a) *Tien Jaren Programma Afval 1992–2002*, AOO 92–12m, The Netherlands

Waste Management Council (1992b) *Milieu-effectrapport Ontwerp Tien Jaren Programma Afval 1992–2002*, AOO 92-02, The Netherlands

Chapter 8

Budhathoki, P (1994) *Organisation and Administrative Procedure*, background report prepared for the IUCN-EIA study

Central Bureau of Statistics (CBS) (1993) *Population Census of Nepal 1991: Social and Economic Characteristics Tables*, Vol 1, Part 8, Kathmandu, Nepal

His Majesty's Government of Nepal (1994) *National Environmental Impact Assessment Guidelines*, National Planning Commission/IUCN–NCS Implementation Project, Kathmandu

His Majesty's Government (HMG) of Nepal, Asian Development Bank and Finnish International Development Agency (1988) *Master Plan for the Forestry Sector*, Ministry of Forests and Soil Conservation, Kathmandu

IUCN/Nepal/Finnish International Development Agency (1995) *EIA of the Bara Forest Management Plan*, IUCN/Nepal

Joshi, M R (1994a) *Forest and Soil Conservation*, background report prepared for the IUCN-EIA Study

Joshi, S P (1994b) *Forest Management*, background report prepared for the IUCN-EIA Study

Kanel, K (1994) *Forest Economics*, background report prepared for the IUCN-EIA Study

Koirala, P (1994) *Socioeconomic Study*, background report prepared for the IUCN-EIA Study

Manushi (1994) *Socioeconomic Study Concerning Participatory Issues in Forest Management and Utilisation of Government Managed Forests in the Terai*, Manushi Group, Kathmandu

McEachern, P, and B Bhandari (1994) *Wetland (Halkhuriya) Study*, background report prepared for the IUCN-EIA Study

National Planning Commission (NPC), Ministry of Forest and Soil Conservation and IUCN (1993) *EIA Guidelines for the Forestry Sector*

Parajuli, D P (1994) *Forest Policy, Legislation and Relevance of EIA*, background report prepared for the IUCN-EIA Study

Pesonen, P (1994) 'The Importance of Terai Natural Forest to Nepal', in *Forest Management Utilisation Development Project*, proceedings of the Terai National Forest Management Seminar

Rautiainen, O (1994) 'Regeneration of Sal: A Myth and an Opportunity', in *Forest Management Utilisation Development Project*, proceedings of the Terai National Forest Management Seminar

Seppanen, H, and K P Acharya (1994) *Operational Forest Management Plan for the Bara District Areas 1994/95–1998/99*, Forest Management Utilisation Project, Kathmandu

Upreti, B K (1994) *Vegetation Study*, background report prepared for the IUCN-EIA Study

Uprety, B N (1994) *Wildlife and Biodiversity*, background report prepared for the IUCN-EIA Study

Wood, C (1988) 'EIA in Plan Making', in P Wathern (ed), *Environmental Impact Assessment: Theory and Practice*, Unwin Hyman, London

Chapter 9

Department of the Environment (DoE) (1990) *This Common Inheritance*, HMSO, London

Department of the Environment (1991) *Policy Appraisal and the Environment*, HMSO, London

Department of the Environment (1992) *Planning Policy Guidance Note 12: Development Plans and Regional Guidance*, HMSO, London

Department of the Environment (1993) *Environmental Appraisal of Development Plans: A Good Practice Guide*, HMSO, London

Department of the Environment (1994) *Environmental Appraisal in Government Departments*, HMSO, London

Hertfordshire County Council (1994) *Structure Plan Review: Environmental Appraisal: Stage 1 Consultation Document*, Hertford

World Commission on Environment and Development (WCED) (1987) *Our Common Future*, Oxford University Press, Oxford

Chapter 10

Engström, C-J (1991) 'The System of Physical Planning and Management of Natural Resources in Sweden', in National Board of Housing and Building *The Integration of Land Use Planning and Environmental Impact Assessment*, Karlskrona

Larsson, B, B-Å Johansson, E Asplund and T Hilding-Rydevik (1993, in Swedish) *The Nobel Railway Through the Town of Karlskoga: Proposal for Comprehensive Plan and Strategic Environmental Assessment*, Municipality of Karlskoga

Municipality of Sollentuna (1993) *Proposal for Comprehensive Plan for Margareteborg in Sollentuna*

Chapter 11

State of California (1986) *The California Environmental Quality Act*, PRC Sec 21000 et seq, Office of Planning and Research, Sacramento, California

San Joaquin County Community Development Department (1992) *Final Environmental Impact Report on the San Joaquin County Comprehensive Planning Program*, ER 91–3, State Clearinghouse No 91012072. The San Joaquin County general plan EIR is being added to a digital library on the environment of California. The complete document, including text, maps and tables will be available over the World Wide Web at: http://elib.cs.berkeley.edu/.

Chapter 12

Commission of the European Communities (CEC) (1992) *Towards Sustainability: Fifth Action Programme on the Environment*, Brussels

European Commission (1993a) *Environmental Profiles for Regional Plans*, Directorate General for Regional Policy, Brussels (unpublished)

European Commission (1993b) *Environmental Appraisal of Regional Plans: Objectives 1 & 2*, Directorate-General for Environment, Nuclear Safety and Civil Protection, (unpublished)

European Commission (1994) *Ireland: Community Support Framework, 1994–99 (Objective 1: Development and Structural Adjustment of Regions Whose Development is Lagging Behind)*, Office for Official Publications of the European Communities, Luxembourg

European Communities (1985) *Council Directive (85/337/EEC) on the Assessment of the Effects of Certain Public and Private Projects on the Environment*, OJ No L175, p 40

European Communities (1988) *Council Regulation (EEC) No 2052/88 on the Tasks of the Structural Funds and Their Effectiveness and on Coordination of Their Activities Bbetween Themselves and with the Operations of the European Investment Bank and the Other Existing Financial Instruments*, OJ No L185, pp 9–20

European Communities (1993) *Council Regulation (EEC) No 2081/93 Amending Regulation (EEC) No 2052/88 on the Tasks of the Structural Funds and Their Effectiveness and on Coordination of Their Activities Between Themselves and with the Operations of the European Investment Bank and the Other Existing Financial Instruments*, OJ L193, pp 5–19

Government of Ireland (1993) *The National Development Plan 1994–1999*, Government Supplies Agency, Dublin

Chapter 13

Bouzaher, A, J F Shogren, D Holtkamp, P Gassman, D Archer, A Carriquiry, R Reese, W H Furtan, R C Izaurralde, and J Kiniry (1995) *Agricultural Policies and Soil Degradation in Western Canada: An Agro-Ecological Assessment*, Policy Branch Technical Reports 1–5, Agriculture and Agri-Food Canada, Ottawa, Canada

Farm Income Protection Act (1991) Statutes of Canada, Chapter 22, Clause 5(2)(b), Ottawa, Canada

Fox, G and M von Massow (1994) *Environmental Assessment of Crop Insurance*, prepared by Price-Waterhouse Management Consultants for Agriculture and Agri-Food Canada, Ottawa, Canada

McRae, T (1995) *Report of the Second National Consultation Workshop on Agri-Environmental Indicators for Canadian Agriculture*, Agriculture and Agri-Food Canada, Ottawa, Canada

Chapter 14

Partidário, MR (1996) 'SEA: Key Issues Emerging from Recent Practice', Environmental Impact Assessment Review, 16 (1), pp 31–55

Thérivel, R (1995) *Environmental Appraisal of Development Plans 1992–1995*, Working Paper No 160, School of Planning, Oxford Brookes University

Index